American Inside Out Evolution

Workbook

Upper Intermediate

Macmillan Education
Companies and representatives throughout the world
American Inside Out Evolution. Workbook Upper Intermediate

Adapted by Petter Maggs and Catherine Smith
Content Writers: Ben Naismith, James Ubriaco and Lavaughn John
Macmillan is a registered trademark.
First edition published 2018

ISBN: 978-607-473-635-9

Based on New American Inside Out Workbook Upper Intermediate
D.R. © Macmillan Publishers, S.A. de C.V. 2010
Published under license from Macmillan Publishers Ltd.

Director of Languages Brazil: Patrícia Souza
Editorial Manager: Patricia Muradas
Art Editor: Jean Aranha
Content Editor: Cintia Zaitune and Larissa Vannucci
Digital Editor: Ana Paula Girardi
Concept design: Martha Tadaieski
Page make-up: Figurattiva Editorial
Illustrations: Gustavo Gialuca
Graphic Production: Kelly Gobbo and Tatiane Romano
Proofreaders: Edward Willson and Larissa Vazquez
Photographic research: Denis Araujo, Jean Aranha and Marcia Sato
Image Processing: Denis Araujo and Jean Aranha
Cover concept and design: Jean Aranha
Cover photo: Songquan Deng | Dreamstime.com

The authors and publishers would like to thank the following for permission to reproduce their photographs:
iStock / batuhan toker p6; Fotoarena / DPA p7; iStock / Ranta Images p11; iStock / martinedoucet p11; iStock / JohnnyGreig p11; Fotoarena/Fox Searchlight Pictures/ Everett Collection p16; iStock / jpkirakun p21; iStock / fakezzz p22; Fotoarena/Alamy p27; iStock / Bet_Noire p28; iStock / serge001 p30; iStock / SeanPavonePhoto p31; iStock / Poike p33; Casa De Lope De Veja,Madrim, Espanha p37; Oxford University Press p38; Harper Collins p38; Darylyn Brooksp38; Fotoarena/Album p40; Fotoarena/Album p40; iStock / diane39 p44; iStock / Steve Debenport p44; iStock / monels p44; iStock / Pgiam p44; iStock / vgajic p45; iStock / GoodLifeStudio p46; iStock / vadimguzhva p48; iStock / PeopleImages p48; iStock / TatyanaGl p48; iStock / fabiodinatale p49; iStock / herraez p49.

CANIEM No. 2275

Macmillan Publishers S.A. de C.V. Insurgentes Sur 1886
Col. Florida, CP 01030
Álvaro Obregón
Ciudad de México
Tel: +52 (55) 5482 2200
elt@grupomacmillan.com

www.grupomacmillan.com
www.macmillan.com.mx
www.macmillanenglish.com

Printed in Brazil

This book was printed in January, 2025 by: Eskenazi Indústria Gráfica Ltda, Avenida Miguel Frias Vasconcelos, 1023 - Jaguaré - São Paulo - SP.

Printed in Brazil. Fourth print. June, 2019.

Contents

1 Impressions

GRAMMAR

1 **Match the verb structures with the examples in the text below.**

a Simple present ___1___
b Present progressive ______
c Simple past ______
d Past progressive ______
e Present perfect simple ______
f Present perfect progressive ______
g Past perfect simple ______
h Past perfect progressive ______

I (1) *live* in a small apartment in New York. I (2) *'ve been studying* management and my course (3) *has* almost *ended*. When I (4) *arrived*, I (5) *'d been planning* to look for a job here, but now I (6) *'m thinking* of moving to Atlanta. I (7) *'d* never *wanted* to live there before, but I (8) *wasn't expecting* to find New York so expensive.

2 **Underline the most appropriate verb form.**

I (1) **am just buying** / **just bought** a really cool pair of blue sunglasses. I (2) **walked** / **was walking** around the mall when I (3) **have seen** / **saw** a new designer store. I (4) **had been looking** / **used to look** for some aviator glasses for ages, and the store (5) **was selling** / **had sold** some very cheaply. I (6) **used to have** / **would have** a very similar pair. I (7) **had always been feeling** / **always feel** so much more comfortable when I (8) **'m wearing** / **have worn** sunglasses.

3 **Complete the pairs of sentences by choosing *So* or *Neither* and filling in the blanks with an auxiliary verb. Three of the pairs of sentences are completely untrue! Which ones?**

a Berlin holds an annual movie festival.
So / **Neither** ___does___ Venice.

b *Star Wars* is one of the most successful movies of all time.
So / **Neither** __________ *Titanic*.

c Nicolas Cage has never won an Oscar®.
So / **Neither** __________ Jodie Foster.

d The directors of *No Country for Old Men* won an Oscar® in 2008.
So / **Neither** __________ Daniel Day-Lewis.

e Angelina Jolie has a famous father.
So / **Neither** __________ Kiefer Sutherland.

f Jennifer Lopez has never been married.
So / **Neither** __________ Antonio Banderas.

g Heath Ledger was not born in America.
So / **Neither** __________ Schwarzenegger.

h Matt Damon trained as a ballet dancer.
So / **Neither** __________ Tom Hanks.

4 **Write responses to the sentences below that are true for you. Use either a phrase with *so* or *neither*, or a phrase with *I* + an auxiliary verb.**

a I love Madonna's music.
So do I. / I don't!

b I've always wanted to be a movie star.
____

c I'd like to have lots and lots of children.
____

d I never watch MTV.
____

e I don't really pride myself on anything.
____

f I'm reading a great book right now.
____

g I used to color my hair.
____

h I've never seen any of Madonna's movies.
____

i I couldn't live without my sneakers.
____

5 **Match the questions with the appropriate tag.**

a	You were born in 1991,	are you?	
b	You're Canadian,	weren't you?	R
c	You aren't married,	can you?	
d	You don't eat meat,	did you?	
e	You have a car,	didn't you?	
f	You lived in Quebec,	do you?	
g	You can't swim,	have you?	
h	You've never worked,	don't you?	
i	You didn't study Art,	aren't you?	

02 **Listen and check your answers. Then listen again and say if these are real questions (with rising intonation) or if they are asking for agreement (falling intonation). Write *R* for rising and *F* for falling intonation in the boxes.**

6 **Complete each sentence with a tag question.**

a She has a baby girl, _doesn't she_ ?
b I didn't promise, ____________ ?
c OK, I forgot to tell you yesterday, but I'm telling you now, ____________ ?
d You've put on a few kilos, ____________ ?
e Her last movie wasn't very good, ____________ ?
f She never writes, ____________ ?
g Nobody wants to look like that, ____________ ?

7 **Rewrite the questions below, beginning with the words given.**

a What kind of salary are you looking for?
Do you know what _kind of salary you are looking for?_
b Which political party do you vote for?
Could you tell me ____________
c Do you work well under stress?
Do you think that ____________
d Have you ever been in trouble with the police?
Do you mind telling me ____________
e What is more important for you: money or job satisfaction?
I'd like to know what ____________
f Are you a "morning person" or an "afternoon person"?
Would you say that ____________
g Do you believe in God?
I'd like to know whether ____________

Which of these questions would you answer truthfully at a job interview?

PRONUNCIATION

03 **Listen to the following mini-conversations. In each dialogue, put a check (✓) next to the speaker (A or B) who sounds more interested.**

a A: I'm working on a magazine feature about elephants.
B: Elephants? Really?
b A: I work for the American Central Bank.
B: Oh, do you?
c A: I'm going to the mall this afternoon.
B: You're not going to Zara, by any chance?
d A: We went clubbing last night.
B: Again?
e A: Don't you think she looks just like Gwyneth Paltrow?
B: More like my mom.
f A: There's baseball on TV tonight.
B: Oh, great!

Practice the mini-conversations. Try to sound as interested as possible.

VOCABULARY

1 **Put the adjectives into two groups.**

~~abrasive~~ charming fake harsh
hearty shrill sparkling strident warm

Usually positive characteristics	Usually negative characteristics
	abrasive

2 **Match the adjectives (a–g) with the nouns (1–7) to make phrases.**

a fake — 1 clothes
b abrasive — 2 eyes
c close-set — 3 hair
d limp — 4 handshake
e scruffy — 5 manner
f shrill — 6 smile
g tousled — 7 voice

a	b	c	d	e	f	g
_6_						

3 **Complete the sentences with the words in the box.**

~~charming~~ designer firm forced
husky impassive spiky staring

a She had a _charming_ manner and we felt very welcome.
b He introduced himself and gave me a ____________ handshake.
c She had an ____________ face and it was impossible to know her feelings.
d He had a ____________ smile and I knew he wasn't really happy.
e She had dark, ____________ eyes and I thought she was a little crazy.
f He had ____________ hair which was colored pink and green.
g She had an attractive, ____________ voice when she sang.
h He always wore ____________ clothes when he went to a nightclub.

4 Underline the correct alternative.

a I'd like to **rearrange** / **repackage** the furniture in the class.

b They managed to **reconsider** / **reconstruct** the economy with help from the World Bank.

c I'm afraid you're going to have to **rethink** / **reunite** your ideas.

d I think you should **reinvent** / **reword** your answer so that it's a little more polite.

e I've heard they're going to **remake** / **reorganize** the movie with American actors.

f My computer crashed and I had to **redo** / **remake** all my work.

g The politician is trying to **relocate** / **repackage** himself as a socialist.

h It's time to **re-examine** / **redraft** all the evidence and find out exactly what happened.

5 Complete the sentences with words from the box.

~~cuff~~ sleeve buckle belt button

a It was just an off-the- *cuff* remark.

b She's almost 100 years old but she's still as bright as a ________ .

c My mother says I'll have to tighten my ________ with all the economic problems these days.

d You have to admit that she wears her heart on her ________ .

e It's really time for her to ________ down and do some work.

6 Match the responses below with the sentences in Exercise 5.

1 But she hasn't stopped spending money, has she?

2 Yes, but I think she should hide her feelings for him a little more.

3 Yes, but it's a shame that he didn't think more before opening his mouth.

4 Yes. Otherwise, she'll never pass her exams.

5 Yes, she's very quick, isn't she?

1	2	3	4	5
c				

7 Underline the correct word to complete the conversation.

Jack: Hey, you'll never (1) **guess** / **know** / **say** who I saw last week.

Megan: Who?

Jack: Nicole Kidman. She's renting a house on my street.

Megan: No! It (2) **can't** / **won't** / **shouldn't** be her. She lives in Australia. You say such stupid things sometimes.

Jack: Calm (3) **about** / **down** / **around** and listen. She's making a movie here.

Megan: I don't believe you!

Jack: Hey! Don't get so worked (4) **on** / **up** / **down**. It's true. I spoke to her.

Megan: Stop it! You're so (5) **angry** / **annoying** / **surprising**. I know it's not true.

Jack: OK, OK. But you believed me when I told you about Johnny Depp.

04 Listen and check.

8 Write the missing letters to complete the conversation.

Megan: Look at (1) t_ _ _ man (2) o_ _ _ there.

Jack: Which one? The (3) o_ _ (4) w_ _ _ the short hair?

Megan: Yes. He's the spitting (5) i_ _ _ _ of Kiefer Sutherland!

Jack: Him? He (6) b_ _ _ _ absolutely no (7) r_ _ _ _ _ _ _ _ _ _ to Kiefer Sutherland!

Megan: Yes, he does. And look! He's got the (8) s_ _ _ distinctive tattoo on his arm. I'd (9) r_ _ _ _ _ _ _ _ that tattoo anywhere.

Jack: I'm sorry. I don't think he (10) l_ _ _ _ anything (11) l_ _ _ Kiefer Sutherland.

Megan: Yes, he does. In fact, I think it's him. He's an amazing-(12) l_ _ _ _ _ _ guy, don't you think?

Jack: Well if that's Kiefer Sutherland, he's changed a lot!

Megan: Hey! He's walking towards us! It really is him!

05 Listen and check.

WRITING

Writing a short biography

Sentence structure and paragraph organization

Spelling

1 **Read the article and choose the best title.**

a As tears go by

b The life of a hippie

c A voice and a life

2 **Use the paragraph plan below to put the paragraphs (a–c) in the correct order.**

Paragraph 1 ☐

Who is he/she? Age?
What is he/she famous for?
How popular is he/she in your country?

Paragraph 2 ☐

What does he/she look like?
Has he/she ever changed his/her appearance or image?
Do you know what he/she has been doing recently?
What is the best thing he/she has ever done?

Paragraph 3 ☐

When did you first become aware of him/her?
Have you ever seen him/her in real life?
How long have you been a fan?
What do you particularly like about him/her?
Is there anything you don't like about him/her?

3 **Divide *Paragraph a* into five sentences.**

4 **Ten of the eleven words below are spelled wrongly. Correct them. You can read the article again to check your answers.**

apeared	beuatifull	consert	diferent
extremly	fasinating	favrite	includeing
intresting	resently	serious	

5 **Write about a famous living person that you like or admire.**

You should use the paragraph plan in Exercise 2 to help you.

Make notes before you start writing.

You should write approximately 180 words.

a

I first discovered her music because my mother used to like it and listen to it when she was cooking about ten years ago, Marianne Faithfull was in concert here, and we went together she was superb I love the way she sings, and she has had such a fascinating life I don't like everything that she has done, but she's always interesting.

b

Marianne Faithfull is a singer and actress who is probably in her 70s now. She is best known for her music, and she has recorded with many different artists, including David Bowie and Metallica. She has also appeared in a number of movies.

c

Faithfull was extremely beautiful when she was young, and she dressed in the hippie clothes that were the fashion among all her friends. She looks more serious now, but she is still very good-looking. She has recently released a new album, *Easy Come Easy Go*. My favorite song of hers is *As Tears Go By*, which she recorded in the 1960s and which was written by Mick Jagger and Keith Richards of The Rolling Stones, and Andrew Oldham, who had "discovered" Marianne. She was dating Mick Jagger at the time.

2 Generations

GRAMMAR

1 Underline the correct alternative.

a Stop it! You're **aiming** / **forcing** / **making** me laugh.
b **Decide** / **Let** / **Offer** me do it for you.
c I can't **afford** / **force** / **let** you to do it, but ...
d Please! Will you **allow** / **avoid** / **make** me to speak?
e I hope your parents don't **enjoy** / **get** / **warn** to hear about that!
f Let's **arrange** / **dread** / **encourage** to meet this weekend.
g Don't even **attempt** / **finish** / **urge** to explain! I won't believe you.
h I don't **aim** / **expect** / **mind** paying.
i Why didn't you **ask** / **hope** / **try** me to do it?

Have you ever said the sentences above, or has anyone ever said them to you (in your own language)? In what circumstances?

2 Put the verbs in parentheses into the correct form.

a I always try to understand (understand) my parents' point of view.
b I avoid ____________ (talk) to my parents about personal things.
c I can't stand ____________ (go) to big family reunions.
d I expect my parents ____________ (help) me financially all my life.
e I enjoy ____________ (spend) time with my parents' friends.
f I have never told my parents ____________ (leave) me alone.
g I never let my parents ____________ (know) all my secrets.
h I often ask my parents ____________ (give) me advice.

Change the sentences above to make them true for you. Check (✓) the sentences that are already true.

____
____
____
____
____
____
____

3 Complete the second sentence so that it means the same as the first.

a They didn't have enough money to buy lots of new clothes.
They couldn't afford to buy lots of new clothes

b They told me that it was a good idea to go to church every week.
They encouraged ____________________________

c They always refused to allow me to bring friends home.
They never let ____________________________

d They insisted on me coming home at ten o'clock every night.
They made ____________________________

e They said that I shouldn't go to nightclubs because they were dangerous.
They warned ____________________________

f My father thought that I should work in his factory.
My father expected ____________________________

g I learned from my parents to respect authority.
My parents taught ____________________________

h I was really nervous about telling my parents that I had a boyfriend.
I was dreading ____________________________

i I succeeded in running away from home when I was 15.
I managed ____________________________

j I made an attempt to live on my own, but it was very hard.
I tried ____________________________

4 **Complete the text with the words in the box.**

about ~~at~~ at for in
of to to with with

Two years ago, I went to a language school in the USA and stayed with a host family. At the time, I was terrible (1) ___at___ English, and it was difficult (2) ________ understand them very well. But they didn't say much anyway, and I had the impression that they weren't very interested (3) ________ me. I was amazed (4) ________ how little they said, even to each other. This was really surprising, because I thought Americans were famous (5) ________ being very communicative. I was very pessimistic (6) ________ my chances of improving my spoken English.

The family really liked potatoes, which we had for dinner almost every day. At least that was better than the boiled fish (which I'm allergic (7) ________) that we had on Fridays. I was afraid (8) ________ saying anything about the food, but one day I'd had enough. I was fed up (9) ________ potatoes! The words poured out of my mouth and I was really impressed (10) ________ my progress in English!

5 **Write the words in order to complete the questions.**

a difficult find get in it morning the to up ?
Do you _find it difficult to get up in the morning?_

b embarrassing English for speak to you ?
Is it ________________________

c email find get irritating it spam to ?
Do you ________________________

d a easy for keep secret to you ?
Is it ________________________

e commericals boring find it on to TV watch ?
Do you ________________________

f amusing at family pictures find it look old to ?
Do you ________________________

Write true answers to the questions.

VOCABULARY

1 **Underline the correct alternative.**

a I'm **dreading** / **avoiding** my parents finding out my exam results.

b She is **aiming** / **arranging** to be a millionaire before she's thirty.

c I **afford** / **avoid** having meetings first thing in the morning.

d Do you think you will **expect** / **manage** to finish all the work on time?

e The coach **urged** / **hoped** his players to attack more in the second half.

f Don't do it, OK? You have been **offered** / **warned**!

g I don't **mind** / **prefer** doing the dishes if you want.

h If we want to help her do well, we should really **decide** / **encourage** her to study more.

2 **Write the words in order to make sayings about family and friendship.**

a at begins charity home
Charity begins at home.

b blood water than thicker is
____

c heart home is is the where
____

d a birds feather flock of together
____

e a company crowd three's two's
____

f another deserves good one turn
____

3 **Match the situations (1–6) with the sayings (a–f) from Exercise 2.**

1 After he won the lottery, a lot of Joe's friends asked him to help them in various ways. But Joe decided, first of all, to help his sister set up her own company. [a]

2 To thank Joe for his generosity, his sister called her company "My Brother Joe." [ ]

3 Joe wanted to celebrate his lottery win with a quiet evening at a restaurant with his girlfriend. Every few minutes, unfortunately, someone came to his table to talk to him. [ ]

4 A few years after becoming a millionaire, Joe found that many of his new friends were also millionaires. [ ]

5 Joe bought a luxury apartment in Manhattan, but after a while he decided to go back and live in his small family home in the town of Woodstock in Vermont. [ ]

6 Back in his hometown, he discovered that he got along better with his sister, brothers, and cousins than he did with his new millionaire friends. [ ]

4 **Match the adjectives in the box with the definitions.**

allergic	amazed	fed up	~~impressed~~
irritating	optimistic	terrible	

a admiring someone or something very much

impressed

b annoyed or bored with something that you feel you have accepted for too long

____

c making you feel annoyed or impatient

____

d very bad in ability

____

e thinking that good things will happen in the future

____

f unable to eat something for medical reasons

____

g very surprised

____

5 **Complete the sentences with adjectives from Exercise 4.**

a Don't ask me to fix the car! I'm absolutely *terrible* at anything mechanical!

b Don't cook fish for him – he's __________ to it.

c I thought I'd done very badly on the exam, but I got 94%. I was __________ at how well I'd done.

d It was an excellent movie. I was really __________ with the acting.

e Let's be __________ about our chances. It'll all be OK.

f Please stop singing that song. I find it really __________ to have to listen to it twenty times a day.

g I'm completely __________ with work. I need a new challenge.

6 **Complete the conversation with the words in the box.**

call	have	help	holler	make
show	~~take~~	welcome		

Marsha: Hello, you must be Darren. Come in, come in. Let me (1) *take* your bag.

Darren: Thanks. That's very kind of you, Mrs. Hoskins.

Marsha: Oh, please (2) __________ me Marsha! Did you (3) __________ a good trip?

Darren: Not too bad, thanks.

Marsha: Glad to hear it. Anyway, (4) __________ to our home. Come into the living room and (5) __________ yourself comfortable.

Darren: Thank you, Mrs. Hoskins.

Marsha: Amanda will be home soon, but before she comes, I'll (6) __________ you around. You'll be in the room next to Amanda's.

Darren: OK, thanks.

Marsha: I'll just go and make us a cup of coffee. And, here, (7) __________ yourself to the cookies.

Darren: Thanks.

Marsha: If there's anything you need while I'm in the kitchen, just (8) __________ .

Darren: OK, Mrs. Hoskins. Thanks.

▶ 06 **Listen and check.**

PRONUNCIATION

1 **Put the words in the box in the correct spaces.**

annoy	~~chase~~	clothes	clown	fake
flight	ground	host	join	wild

a /eɪ/ gray, say, *chase* , __________

b /aɪ/ buy, try, __________ , __________

c /ɔɪ/ boy, toy, __________ , __________

d /oʊ/ go, know, __________ , __________

e /aʊ/ how, now, __________ , __________

▶ 07 **Listen and check. Repeat the words.**

2 **Underline the word in each group that has a different vowel sound.**

a host lost most

b near wear year

c five give wives

d how low now

e gave have save

▶ 08 **Listen and check.**

LISTENING

1 09 **Cover the listening script on the right. Listen and look at the pictures of three women when they were 21 years old. Match the speakers (1–3) with the pictures (a–c).**

a 

Lalita Parikh, 43, has a 21-year-old daughter, Akhila

b 

Christine Rance, 56, has a 21-year-old daughter, Leia

c 

Mary Billups, 65, has a 21-year-old step-daughter, Zoë

Speaker 1: Picture ______
Speaker 2: Picture ______
Speaker 3: Picture ______

2 **Listen again and check (✓) the topics that each speaker mentions. Some topics are mentioned by more than one speaker.**

	entertainment	marriage	politics	money	studies	work
Speaker 1						
Speaker 2						
Speaker 3						

3 **Find the idioms (a–f) in the listening script and underline the best definition.**

a a dead-end job (Speaker 1) *a bad job / a good job*

b not all they're cracked up to be (Speaker 1) *not as bad as people claim / not as good as people claim*

c messed up (Speaker 2) *caused things to go well / go wrong*

d handed to them on a plate (Speaker 2) *made very easy for them / made very hard for them*

e make ends meet (Speaker 3) *get a job / survive financially*

f the best of both worlds (Speaker 3) *a situation where two cultures meet / a situation where you have two very different advantages*

1 When I was my step-daughter's age, I remember my own parents saying to me all the time "You've never had it so good," but I could never really understand what was so good about it. There was the music - the Beatles and the Rolling Stones - and the new fashions, mini-skirts of course, but they didn't really change much for most of us. I got a job when I was eighteen, a real dead-end job. I was working in a horrible office, nine-to-five, or more like eight-to-six, and in the evenings we had dinner and watched TV - black and white, of course. I'd taken a three-month secretarial course and I never had the chance to go to college like my step-daughter. I think she's lucky. The sixties weren't all they're cracked up to be! She has so much more freedom than I ever had. I'm not complaining, but I wish I'd been born twenty years later. Who knows how my life would have been different?

2 When I was my daughter's age, things were very different. We didn't spend all our time shopping or watching TV like my daughter and her friends seem to do all the time. I mean, don't get me wrong, I love my daughter, but she doesn't seem to care about anything that matters. I suppose the world was very different then. It was an important time for the Civil Rights movement and we were much more political. Most weekends, we were at demonstrations. I even saw Martin Luther King speak. We felt the government had messed up. Then again, I'm not so sure that things are a lot better now. Kids these days don't have it so easy. I mean, everything costs so much money. Nothing is handed to them on a plate.

3 When I was my daughter's age, I hadn't been in the USA long. Maybe for a little more than a year. Actually, I came over here to get married and the first few years it was hard to make ends meet, with my husband trying to set up his business. Basically, I was spending most days with my husband's family, but when our daughter came along, there wasn't time for very much. Now that she is grown up, we would like her to meet a nice boy and get married. We sometimes suggest nice boys that she will like, but she is not interested. She has finished her college studies and she says that she wants to have her career. Obviously, we want her to have the best of both worlds, work and family, but we worry that she will wait too long before she settles down.

3 Gold

GRAMMAR

1 **Read the conversation and complete the reported speech sentences using the verbs in parentheses. You may need to add the personal pronouns *he*, *she*, or *they*.**

Chris: Guess what? I just won the lottery.
Sarah: How much did you win?
Chris: 10,000 dollars!
Sarah: What are you going to do with it?
Chris: I don't know! I think I'll buy a new car, to begin with.
Sarah: That'll use up most of the money, won't it?
Chris: Yeah, but I want to keep a little bit to spend on a vacation.
Sarah: A vacation?
Chris: Yeah, do you want to come to the Bahamas?
Sarah: Wow! The Bahamas! I'd love to! When are we going?
Chris: What are you doing next week?

a Chris called Sarah to tell her that he had just won (just / win) the lottery.
b Sarah asked him how much ________ (win) and what ________ (do) with it.
c At first he said ________ (not know), but he thought ________ (buy) a new car.
d Sarah told him that buying a car ________ (use up) most of the money.
e But Chris said ________ (want) to spend some on a vacation.
f He asked Sarah if ________ (want) to go with him.
g She loved the idea and asked him when ________ (go).
h Chris asked her what ________ (do) the following week.

2 **Write what the people said.**

a Chris told Sarah he'd gotten the tickets.
"I got the tickets."
b Sarah asked if she could see them.
____
c Sarah asked when they were leaving.
____
d Chris said she had two days to get ready.
____
e Sarah asked if she needed to bring any money.
____
f Chris said that he would pay for everything.
____
g Sarah said she was going to buy some new clothes.
____
h She asked him if he wanted to go with her.
____
i He said that he'd wait for her at home.
____

3 **Correct the mistake in each of these sentences. Ignore the italics.**

a If I ~~am~~ was / were the president of my country, I'd spend more money on *the environment*.
b If I did ever had the chance, I'd *take a year off and go traveling*.
c If I could live anywhere in the world, I'd probably bought *a beach villa in the Caribbean*.
d If I didn't need to *learn English*, I would stop a long time ago.
e If I didn't have to *go to work tomorrow*, I would have stayed at home.
f If I had been good at *math*, I would have *study it at college*.
g If I was doing more *exercise* when I was younger, I would be *a lot healthier* now.
h If I'd been born with very rich parents, I wouldn't *doing this job*.

Change the words in italics to make the sentences true for you.

4 **Make one conditional sentence with *if* by joining the pairs of sentences.**

a I didn't study hard enough at school. I don't have a good job.

If I studied harder at school, I'd have a better job.

b It's not made of real gold. It's not worth a lot.

______

c They cornered the market. So they put up the price.

______

d He has a talent for seeing a gap in the market. He has made millions.

______

e She didn't realize it was valuable. She gave it away.

______

f My time is so precious. That's why I didn't speak to them.

______

g I was working late. I missed the movie.

______

h I didn't know you were coming. That's why I didn't come to meet you.

______

VOCABULARY

1 **Cross out the noun in each group which is not used with the verb in bold.**

a **have** a talk / a duty / office
b **make** a trash / a loss / a mess
c **take** office / a fortune / responsibility
d **have** a vision / difficulty / action
e **make** sense / a risk / a fuss
f **take** way / sugar / an exam

2 **Complete the sentences using *have*, *make*, or *take* in the correct form.**

a The Californian gold rush _took_ place in 1849.
b Thousands of people find it very hard to ______ a living.
c Why don't you ______ your father's advice and find yourself a part-time job?
d If you want to ______ money, you have to be ready to ______ risks.
e I need to ______ some time to think before I accept your offer. Can I get back to you tomorrow?
f Oh, come on, there's no need to get angry. We were only ______ fun.
g Don't panic. Don't look down, just ______ a deep breath and then jump.
h Small businesses often struggle to ______ a profit in the first years.

3 **Match the two halves of the expressions.**

a	a half-baked	1	couple of minutes
b	a steady stream	2	your while
c	digest	3	your time
d	food	4	more profitably
e	spare a	5	idea
f	spend the	6	for thought
g	trickle	7	the information
h	use your time	8	evening
i	waste	9	of people
j	worth	10	slowly

a	b	c	d	e	f	g	h	i	j
5									

4 **Match the expressions in Exercise 3 with the metaphors below.**

a ideas = food

_a / 5_ ______ ______

b movement = water

______ ______

c time = money

______ ______ ______ ______ ______

5 **Use the expressions from Exercise 3 to complete the sentences below. You may need to make some changes to the verbs.**

a There was ___a steady stream of people___ coming in through the gates of the park.

b The situation was very complicated, and it took some time for me to ______________ ______________ .

c You're going to have to learn to ______________ ______________ or you'll find yourself failing all your exams.

d The opening speech was very powerful and gave us all a lot of ______________ .

e Do you think my plan could possibly work, or is it just ______________ ?

f Excuse me, do you think you could ______________ ?

g We ______________ watching old movies and eating popcorn.

h We sat and watched the rain ______________ ______________ down the window.

i If you think you're going to persuade me to take up judo, you're ______________ !

j Can you sit down and help me with this exercise? I'll make it ______________ !

6 **Complete the texts with the words in the boxes.**

a rainy day
blow
breadwinner
debt
living
~~loaded~~
peanuts
splash out

A: I wish I was (1) ___loaded___ . I'd (2) ______________ on all kinds of things: clothes, shoes, eating out, going on vacation. If I didn't have a family to take care of and a home to run, I'd love to just (3) ______________ all my money on an around-the-world trip, or something. But as it is, I have to work hard just to earn a basic (4) ______________ for me and my family. It's really difficult these days, being the main (5) ______________ . My husband works part-time when he can. He works for a truck company, but they pay him (6) ______________ . Some months we manage to put a little money in the bank, you know, saving for (7) ______________ , but most of it goes towards paying off our (8) ______________ – that and feeding eight mouths!

budget
hard
made
pricey
range
stretch
worth

B: It isn't (1) ______________ much. You know, he isn't (2) ______________ of money. I know he wanted to buy something a little more (3) ______________ , but he's a little (4) ______________ up right now and a real diamond would have been way out of his price (5) ______________ . And anyway, we want to spend a little more on the wedding itself, you know, have a big party, invite all our family and friends. We don't have a huge (6) ______________ , but I think we can (7) ______________ it to a buffet lunch and some tea. After all, you only get married once, don't you?

▶ 10 **Listen and check.**

7 **Write the words in order to make sentences.**

a looking for colorful was I a little more something

___I was looking for something a little more colorful.___

b wondering have something less you a little formal was if I might

____

c thinking more was something exciting I of a little

____

d something I a little hoping less was for expensive

____

e older a little I'd looks like that something

____

f prefer more I'd fun something a little

____

PRONUNCIATION

1 **Put the words in the box in the appropriate space.**

deluge	special	stretch	treasure	wealthy	whether

a /θ/ thought ______________

b /ð/ although ______________

c /ʒ/ decision ______________

d /ʃ/ collection ______________

e /tʃ/ rich ______________

f /dʒ/ range ______________

11 Listen and check. Repeat the words.

2 **12 Look at the underlined letters, listen to the recording, and write the correct symbol.**

a fortune, future ____

b genuine, village ____

c decision, disillusion ____

d theft, worth ____

e direction, precious ____

f breathe, rather ____

WRITING

Writing a story from pictures
Time expressions
Using adverbs

1 **Read the story and underline the best linkers. Sometimes more than one is possible. Ignore the italics.**

On Christmas Eve, Mrs. Clare was doing some last-minute shopping at her local mall (1) **as** / **until** / **when** she walked past a store selling lottery tickets. She decided to buy one for her son. It was getting late, so, (2) **as soon as** / **before** / **while** she bought the ticket, she rushed home to wrap her gifts and put them under the Christmas tree.

(3) **As** / **During** / **While** she was wrapping her son's gift, she slipped the lottery ticket into the package. And (4) **after** / **then** / **when** she forgot all about it. On Christmas Day, her son and daughter-in-law came to her house. They all sat around the tree and opened their gifts. Mrs. Clare had *totally* forgotten about the lottery ticket, and (5) **after** / **as soon as** / **during** her son had opened his gift and thanked his mom, he threw the wrapping paper in the trash can.

A few days later, Mrs. Clare and her son, Jack, were having coffee together downtown. (6) **Before** / **When** / **While** they were talking, a story came on the local news. It said that the winning ticket for the Christmas lottery had been sold in their local store. *Apparently* no one had claimed the winnings.

"Look," said Jack, "that's the store where you usually buy your tickets. And the winning number is the same as my birthday!" *Suddenly*, Mrs. Clare remembered her son's second Christmas gift. "Oh, no!" she cried, jumping out of her seat.

She explained what had happened to her son, and (7) **during** / **until** / **while** the endless ride home on the bus, the two tried to remember what they had done with the wrapping paper. (8) **As soon as** / **Just as** / **When** they got home, Mrs. Clare and Jack ran to the trash can and *frantically* started emptying it, checking every single piece of wrapping paper, (9) **as** / **before** / **until**, *finally*, they found it: the winning ticket!

2 **Look at the words in italics in the story. Find replacements for them in the box.**

at last	completely	desperately	it seemed	just then

3 **Look at the pictures below. They tell another story of a lucky lottery ticket. Write the story. Use about 180 words. Use the words in the box to help you. Remember to use appropriate time linkers and adverbs.**

gas station	glove compartment	papers	new owner	check	juice

4 Challenge

GRAMMAR

1 Underline the correct verb form.

a I **had always wanted** / **was always wanting** to visit Alaska since I was a young boy and **saw** / **was seeing** a movie about it at school.

b When my turn **came** / **had come**, I **just closed** / **was just closing** my eyes and **jumped** / **was jumping**.

c We **had prepared** / **had been preparing** for the trip for over three months. I was so disappointed when they **canceled** / **were canceling** it.

d I **didn't ever do** / **had never done** anything like that before.

e I **was waiting** / **had been waiting** for this moment for so long. But now that it **finally arrived** / **had finally arrived**, I **didn't know** / **hadn't known** what to do!

f We **were getting** / **had gotten** ready to leave when the phone **rang** / **was ringing** and Phil **told** / **was telling** us the terrible news: someone **stole** / **had stolen** our boat!

2 Add ten missing auxiliary verbs (***had***, ***hadn't***, or ***was***) to the text. The first one has been done for you.

Aron Ralston (had) been climbing in a remote canyon in Arizona when disaster struck. He climbing down a particularly narrow part when a huge rock fell and trapped his arm. As he been climbing on his own, there was no one to help him. And he knew that no one would think of looking for him there because he told anyone where he going. He brought his cell phone with him, so he couldn't call for help. He waited for five long days, but no one came to find him. By the fifth day, he lost all sensation in his arm. He realized that he had no choice. He would have to cut his arm off at the elbow in order to save his life. Once he cut off his arm, he managed to climb to the floor of the canyon. As he walking out of the canyon, he met a group of people who been hiking in the area. They called for help and a helicopter soon arrived to take him to a nearby hospital.

13 Listen and check.

3 Write the words in order to complete the questions.

a Aron had when doing happened accident been the ?
What had Aron been doing when the accident happened?

b him for come hadn't look anyone to ?
Why ______

c help called he for hadn't ?
Why ______

d canyon had long he waited in the ?
How ______

e to done away he had get ?
What ______

f hikers met doing when he had been the he ?
What ______

4 Answer the questions from Exercise 3. Use full sentences.

a He had been climbing in a remote canyon.

b ______

c ______

d ______

e ______

f ______

5 Underline the correct verb form.

a I'll **be finishing** / **have finished** this *page before I go to bed*.

b I'll **be going** / **have gone** out with friends *on Thursday night*.

c I'll **be working** / **have worked** hard *all weekend*.

d I'll **be having** / **have had** dinner *by the time you get home*.

e I'll **be getting** / **have gotten** a new job *by this time next month*.

f I won't **be going** / **have gone** away on vacation again *for at least six months*.

g I won't **be playing** / **have played** any sports *this evening*.

h I'll **be getting** / **have gotten** married and **having** / **had** three kids *by the time I'm thirty*.

Change the words in italics to make the sentences true for you.

6 Complete the text using the future progressive or the future perfect form of the verb in parentheses.

I can see a lot of hard work in the future, and you (1) ___will/'ll be doing___ (do) a lot of traveling for your job. But it'll be worth it. By the time you're twenty-five, you (2) ______ (start) your own company. By the time you're thirty, you (3) ______ (make) your first million. And you (4) ______ (fall) in love at least three times. The third time will be the real thing. Fifteen years from now, you (5) ______ (give up) your job and you (6) ______ (live) in a big house in the country. You (7) ______ (change) your lifestyle completely. You and your husband (8) ______ (run) a small farm and taking care of your five children.

14 Listen and check.

PRONUNCIATION

1 15 Listen to the recording and underline the word in italics that is more stressed.

a I definitely don't *feel up to* it.

b You'll soon *shake it off*.

c I think I'm *coming down with* something.

d The children *wore me out*.

e The smell really *put me off*.

f My son looks like my husband, but he *doesn't take after him* in other ways.

2 16 Listen and practice saying the sentences below. Put the stress on the underlined phrases.

a I'm going to cut down a little on candy.

b I can't do it without you!

c I can't keep up with all my work.

d Why don't you come up with a better idea?

e Let's put it off until tomorrow.

VOCABULARY

1 Complete the sentences with the words in the box.

deal genuine ~~imminent~~ interest obscenely particularly shambolic

a The team prepared themselves for their ___imminent___ departure to the North Pole.

b The whole trip was incredibly badly organized – ______ , in fact.

c The expedition created a huge amount of media ______ .

d The leaders of the expeditions were offered a very generous book ______ upon their return.

e It is my ______ belief that anyone who risks their life for a sport is completely crazy.

f Only the ______ rich can afford to have a private jet.

g He's a ______ gifted pianist.

2 Complete the sentences with the correct form of the word in parentheses.

a She was very ___self-conscious___ and hated speaking in public. (conscious)

b The trip had been very ______ . Everyone had had a good time. (enjoy)

c The food was very good and the price was fairly ______ . (reason)

d It takes a lot of ______ to quit smoking. (discipline)

e He suffers from very low ______ . He just doesn't believe in himself. (esteem)

f The government wants to make adult education more ______ to people who work full-time. (access)

g He used to work for himself as a ______ builder before he became an Arctic explorer. (employ)

h The stress was getting ______ , so she left her job. (bear) i The key to success is self-belief. If you believe something is ________________, then you will achieve it. (achieve)

j It'll take some organizing, but I think it's ________________. (do)

3 Match the definitions with the words you wrote in Exercise 2.

a embarrassed or worried about how you look or what people think of you *self-conscious*

b the feeling that you are as important as other people and deserve to be treated well ________________

c gives you pleasure ________________

d possible for you to do (two words) ________________; ________________

e so extreme that you can't deal with it ________________

f with an expected range ________________

g easy to get or use ________________

h the ability to control your behavior so that you do what you should do ________________

i working for yourself ________________

4 Complete the expressions with the words in the box.

into	jammed	load	no
~~of~~	out	slow	undo

a in charge *of*: having control over someone/something and being responsible for them

b the gun ________: the gun didn't work

c ________ way: used for emphasizing that something isn't true or possible

d figure ________: be able to understand or solve a problem

e go into ________ motion: appear to move more slowly than in real life

f ________ the gun: put bullets into the gun

g swing ________ action: start doing something quickly and efficiently

h ________ the zipper: open the zipper

5 Use expressions from Exercise 4 to complete the text below. Make any necessary changes.

He heard a strange noise outside the tent. He lay there trying to (1) *figure out* what it was, then he slowly (2) ________________ of the tent door. He quietly (3) ________________ and pointed it at the darkness. He was (4) ________________ the camp that night, and there was (5) ________________ he was going to let someone steal their food or equipment. Suddenly, a dark shadow jumped out of the trees; it was a lion. He quickly (6) ________________. He tried to fire his gun, but (7) ________________. Everything seemed to (8) ________________.

He picked up a stick and started shouting wildly. The lion stopped, looked at him, and then turned to go away.

▶ 17 **Listen and check.**

6 Underline the correct verb.

a I don't really <u>**feel**</u> / **keep** up to doing any exercise today. Can we put it off until tomorrow?

b Jamie's incredible; he **gives** / **picks** things up so quickly. He learned to surf in a day!

c I'm really trying hard to **give** / **pick** up chocolate. I eat way too much, and it's really bad for me.

d He walked out of the door on to the street and **felt** / **lit** up his last cigarette.

e What does this mean?
I don't know. **Look** / **Take** it up in a dictionary!

f Hey, can you slow down a little, please? I can't **come** / **keep** up with you! You're running too fast.

g Quick! I need to **come** / **take** up with a good excuse for not playing soccer tonight!

h Have you ever thought about **giving** / **taking** up a new sport?

7 Write the words in bold in the correct order.

a I'm not feeling very well. I think I'm **down coming with** something. *coming down with*

b Learning the facts about smoking really **off me put**. ________________

c I'm getting really fed up with this cold. I've been trying to **off it shake** for weeks.
____

d Have you seen Jim's dad? He really **him after takes**. They look exactly alike.
____

e I'm really sorry; I forgot all about the tennis match. I didn't mean to **you down let**.
____

f Give her time. She'll **over get it** soon enough.
____

g Yes, that's really a mystery. We'll have to **into look it**. ________________

h I've tried giving it up, but I really don't think I can **it without do**. ________________

8 Write the words in order to make sentences.

a happens when horrible that It's
It's horrible when that happens.

b right serves you It
____

c blame got You've yourself only to
____

d home were if go I you I'd
____

e death look You like over warmed
____

LISTENING

1 18 **Kandi Wright is a snake handler. She is trying to break the world record for living in a cage with poisonous snakes. Cover the listening script on the right, listen to an interview with Kandi, and answer the questions.**

a Why is she doing it?

b What does she say is the most difficult thing about the experience?

c Does she get bored?

d Does she think she'll be able to break the record?

2 **Listen again. Are the sentences true (T) or false (F)?**

a A man in Zimbabwe had recently succeeded in breaking the record. T

b Her friend suggested that Kandi should try to break the record too. ☐

c Kandi has been in the snake cage for more than two months. ☐

d She doesn't get a lot of visitors. ☐

e A snake bit her on her hand. ☐

f She finds it really hard to stay in shape. ☐

g She spends a lot of time working on her computer. ☐

h She's looking forward to getting out of the cage. ☐

3 **Match the verbs on the left with their collocations on the right.**

a do	an idea
b give someone	a new record
c go	money
d stay	for a walk
e raise	in shape
f set	some exercise

Check your answers in the listening script.

Interviewer: So, Kandi, what gave you the idea for the record attempt in the first place?

Kandi: Well, it all started as a joke. A friend said she'd seen something on the internet about a man in Zimbabwe who'd set a new record for living in a box with 40 poisonous snakes to raise money for a children's charity. We all thought he must have been crazy. But then I started thinking about it, and the idea grew on me. I thought, I could do that - I could break his record. It'd be a great way to raise the profile of Marlton Wildlife Park - you know - get some media interest. So I suggested it - and well, here I am! Day 75, with another 45 to go!

Interviewer: So, how's it been so far? What's been the most difficult thing to get used to?

Kandi: Well, obviously I'm a snake handler - that's my job - so it wasn't difficult getting used to the snakes, but it was difficult getting used to the confined space of my "box" - not being able to go out, not being able to go for a walk, not being able to go back to the comfort of my home at night.

Interviewer: So, what do you do all day? How do you keep yourself from getting bored?

Kandi: Bored? I never get the time! I get tons of visitors - schoolkids, tourists, that kind of thing. I show them the snakes, we talk through this open window here. And then there's the snake page on the park's website - that keeps me really busy. People write in with questions about the snakes - what they eat, where they sleep, if I've been bitten.

Interviewer: And have you?

Kandi: No - not yet! But I did step on one of the mambas one day - poor thing. It was so scared it bit my boot - luckily it's a very strong boot, so its teeth didn't get through to my foot - but I learned to be more careful about where I put my feet after that!

Interviewer: You look like you're in pretty good shape. How do you stay in shape in here? Do you get to do any exercise?

Kandi: Yeah, sure. I've got a running machine in the corner over there. I spend an hour on it in the morning and another 40 minutes or so every evening. It's never been so easy to keep to a fitness regime!

Interviewer: So, what are your plans for the next 45 days? Do you think you'll be able to make it?

Kandi: Sure, no problem. It's just a question of time - and of concentrating on now and not the future - on what I'm doing now and not what I'll be doing when I get out! That just makes the wait seem even longer!

Interviewer: Well, thanks for talking to us, Kandi, and good luck with the next 45 days.

5 Ritual

GRAMMAR

1 **Change the verbs in bold into the simple present where possible.**

I've got a really boring report to write this weekend, and I know what'll happen. The same thing that always happens. I (1) **'ll find** all kinds of little tasks to distract me. I (2) **'ll decide** that it's the perfect time to write all those emails to long lost friends, or I (3) **'ll clear** out the inbox on my cell phone. And I'm sure this time (4) **will be** no different. I (5) **probably won't get** down to work today until I've cleaned the house from top to bottom. Sometimes, when I'm feeling really stressed, I (6) **'ll do** some cooking. At other times I (7) **'ll spend** hours just staring out of the window. Like today. Oh well, I'd better stop wasting time, I suppose, or this report (8) **will never get** written!

2 **Complete the text with *used to* or *didn't use to*.**

Weddings (1) ___used to___ be much simpler in my day. People (2) ________ spend so much money on them, for one thing. And they certainly (3) ________ go abroad to get married. They (4) ________ get married in the local church, and then they (5) ________ invite the guests to a very simple reception afterwards. They (6) ________ have a cake, of course, and possibly some speeches, but they (7) ________ party into the early hours of the morning like they do today.
I (8) ________ like the simple, old-fashioned weddings much more.

3 **Look at the text in Exercise 2 again. Where is it possible to replace *used to / didn't use to* with *would / wouldn't*?**

1 not possible
2 wouldn't
3 ________
4 ________
5 ________
6 ________
7 ________
8 ________

4 **Complete this conversation between two friends with an appropriate form of the verb in parentheses. Use *will* or *would* whenever possible.**

Jayne: Do you remember Bill? He (1) ___used to be___ (be) a real terror in school. Do you remember how he (2) ________ (chase) the girls in the schoolyard?
And what about the day when he (3) ________ (find) a frog and (4) ________ (try) to put it down the back of your shirt?

Becky: Yes, of course I do, how could I forget! And, he and his friends (5) ________ (hide) behind the bathrooms, and they (6) ________ (always / get) caught by the principal ...

Jayne: Yeah, and they (7) ________ (have to) do extra homework for a week!

Becky: So what made you bring him up in the conversation?

Jayne: Well, I (8) ________ (see) him a couple of months ago in a café, and we (9) ________ (have) a drink and talked. He hasn't changed that much. He still tells terrible jokes, but, to be fair to him, he (10) ________ (always / pay) for the drinks ...

Becky: "Always," you say?

Jayne: Yeah, we've been seeing a lot of each other. We usually go to the movies once or twice a week, and sometimes we (11) ________ (play) a game of squash or tennis.

Becky: Hmm ... is it getting serious?

Jayne: I'm not sure. You can judge for yourself. He's meeting us later!

19 **Listen and check.**

5 **Correct the mistakes in six of the sentences below. Check (✓) the sentences that are correct.**

a Could you remember locking the door on your way out this morning, please?
Could you remember to lock the door ...

b Do you remember to tell me that I was the only person in your life?
___

c I bet you forgot to bring the money, didn't you?
___

d It's so long ago that I've completely forgotten to say that. Did I really?
___

e She didn't stop insulting me all evening.
___

f They stopped for a minute getting some money out at the bank on the way to the movies.
___

g This season, I'm going to try winning both the 100 and 200 meters.
___

h Try to cook it in oil – it'll taste a lot better.
___

PRONUNCIATION

1 ▶ 20 **Listen and repeat the phrases below. Make sure that you stress the underlined words.**

a I can't stand it
b as for me
c it's so annoying
d it makes me sick
e here it is

2 **Underline one word that is normally stressed in the phrases below.**

a just the two of us
b it gets on my nerves
c I find it irritating
d it's all in the mind
e from what I can understand
f it drives me crazy

▶ 21 **Listen and check.**

VOCABULARY

1 **Complete the texts with the words in the box.**

came across	crazy	derive	immune	~~jinxed~~	outfit	renowned	rituals	striding	upper hand

a I'm not usually superstitious, but you know how sometimes you feel like you've been (1) *jinxed* – you know, you feel like everything's going wrong? Like today, for example. I was (2) ___ confidently down the street on my way to work. I was feeling good in a new (3) ___ that I was wearing for the first time. Then a car drove right through a big puddle and splashed me with dirty water from head to foot.

b Most people's superstitions (4) ___ from a basic insecurity: from a need to be in control and to have the (5) ___ in difficult situations. Many (6) ___ sports people have personal (7) ___ that they have to perform before a big game. Not even politicians are (8) ___ to superstition. One leading politician admitted to always wearing mismatched socks on election day. He asked us not to give his name in case he (9) ___ as being a little (10) ___!

2 **Write the missing letters to complete the collocations.**

a I settled down on the couch with a mug of hot chocolate and a c *ozy* blanket.
b I felt a sudden u_ _ _ to get up and sing.
c He was furious. He strode out of the room and s_ _ _ _ed the door behind him.
d He reached into his pocket, took out a box of m_ _ _ _ _ _, and lit the candle.
e He passed his driving test on his f_ _ _ _ try.
f I'm sorry, we have a rule about d_ _ _ _ _ _ _ animals – strictly no pets allowed.
g Her husband worked in the US Air F_ _ _ _ and was often away from home.
h He took the corner at b_ _ _ _ _ _ _ _ speed and almost fell off his bike.

3 Underline the correct form of the verb. In one sentence, both verbs may be correct.

a I really feel like I deserve **doing** / **to do** something special this weekend – I've been working so hard all week.

b If I can manage **getting** / **to get** the day off on Monday, I could go away for a couple of days.

c I'd love **going** / **to go** away somewhere – Boston, maybe.

d I like **visiting** / **to visit** new places, and I've never been to Boston before.

e I'd like **going** / **to go** by train.

f I enjoy **being** / **to be** able to see the countryside.

g I can't stand **flying** / **to fly**. I hate airports and waiting around.

h There'll probably be lots of extra work waiting for me when I get back. But I don't intend **getting** / **to get** stressed out about it now!

i All I want **doing** / **to do** is take it easy and relax.

4 Complete the sentences with the words in the box.

~~complaining~~ go insist keeps mad telling

I share an office with a woman who is always (1) *complaining* ! When she arrives in the morning, she'll (2) ____________ on opening all the windows, and then she'll (3) ____________ on and on about how cold it is! She (4) ____________ leaving half-finished cups of coffee on the desk, but then she'll get (5) ____________ at me if I knock them over. She's always (6) ____________ me what to do, but she never seems to get any work done herself!

22 Listen and check.

5 Write the words in order to complete the sentences.

a what people tell to me do when it

I hate *it when people tell me what to do.*

b shout when me people annoys

It really ______________________________

c desk most annoys messy me is that a

The thing ______________________________

d waiting it keep stand people me when

I can't ______________________________

e nobody irritating listens me when to it

I find ______________________________

f nerves get manners my on really

Bad ______________________________

g weekend rains annoying so when it the on

It's ______________________________

h drive crazy some people makes me

The way ______________________________

WRITING

Writing an email of complaint
Formal expressions

1 **Put the email in the correct order.**

a Dear Mr. Gammack,

b Further to our telephone conversation, you are aware that over forty of our guests suffered food poisoning, caused directly by the food you provided, and had to be hospitalized.

c I am writing in connection with the catering services which you provided on October 27 for my daughter, Benita Molly Shepherd's wedding.

d To add insult to injury, on my way to the hospital, I was presented, by one of your staff, with a bill which was $12,000 over the agreed price. Under the circumstances, I think my reaction was understandable. I also think a court of law would agree with me.

e Having taken all of the above into consideration, I have now spoken with my lawyer. You will be hearing from her in due course.

f Your staff, furthermore, were clearly untrained and unsuitable for this type of work. They provoked a fight when the ambulance arrived, as a result of which my son-in-law, Mr. Vinnie Wiseman, was later arrested.

g Yours sincerely,

h Stephen Shepherd

1	2	3	4	5	6	7	8
a							

2 **Find and underline phrases in the email that mean the same as the following.**

a with reference to

b as a direct result of

c above the sum in the contract

d when the time is right

e moreover

f inappropriate for the job

3 **Complete the sentences with a phrase from the box.**

apology	a full refund	I will expect
legal advice	the matter	your life

a If I do not hear from you within ten days, I will be obliged to take ________________ on this matter.

b I look forward to receiving ________________ as soon as possible.

c I trust that we will be able to settle ________________ amicably.

d I look forward to receiving an email of ________________ .

e ________________ substantial compensation and a full apology.

4 **You work in the complaints department of a small company. Put the sentences from Exercise 3 in order from *most threatening* to *least threatening*.**

most threatening ☐ ☐ ☐ ☐ ☐ least threatening

5 **Imagine you are the father of the bride in the story below. The wedding was canceled because of the problems with the car and the driver. Write your email to the manager of Limo Car Hire.**

6 Eat

GRAMMAR

1 Change the present perfect progressive to the present perfect simple in the four sentences where this is necessary. Check (✓) the sentences that are correct.

a I've just been listening to the radio. ✓
b I've always been hating fish.
c I've been being a vegetarian for about ten days.
d I've been feeling a little tired for the last few days.
e I've been doing the first three exercises in class.
f I've been having the same phone for years.
g I've been studying English for five years.
h I've been looking forward to finishing this exercise.

Change the sentences to make them true for you.

2 Look at the picture and put the verbs in parentheses into the present perfect simple or the present perfect progressive.

a They _have / 've finished_ (finish) work for the evening.
b I'm pretty sure they ________________ (cook).
c They ________________ (have) two accidents in the kitchen.
d The one with the mustache ________________ (eat) spaghetti.
e They ________________________ (probably receive) a few complaints from the customers.
f I think they ____________________ (talk) about what went wrong.

3 Correct one mistake in each paragraph.

a Helen has been working for the government for the last six months. She ~~has~~ got the job by replying to an advertisement online. She's already met the president twice.
b Callum has been not studying much recently. He failed three exams at the end of last year. He's only been to school three or four times since then.
c Julie has been dating Jeff for almost a year. They met in a café downtown. She hasn't tell her parents yet.
d Alyson has painting her house. She started last month, but she hasn't made much progress yet.
e Jamie has been living with his father for about five months. His parents separated, and he has only saw his mother a few times since then.
f Dan and Ursula have been get ready for their wedding. They announced the date three years ago. They've almost finished their preparations.

4 Put the verbs in parentheses into the simple past, the present perfect simple, or the present perfect progressive.

Jane: You're looking happy. What's going on?
Dick: Well, you know how I (1) _'ve been working_ (work) part-time in the evenings at the Red Hot Burger?
Jane: Yes, that's right. You (2) ________________ (do) that for about four weeks now.
Dick: Yeah, it was about a month ago that I (3) ________________ (start). Anyway, guess what?
Jane: What? You (4) ________________ (get paid)?
Dick: Yes, yesterday actually. But, no, it's not that. I (5) ________________ (be promoted). They (6) ________________ (make) me the Team Leader.
Jane: Oh, good news. What does "Team Leader" mean, exactly?
Dick: It means that I (7) ________________ (accept) management responsibilities. They (8) ________________ (give) me a red badge to wear.
Jane: You (9) ________________ (move) up in the world!

▶ 23 **Listen and check.**

5 Put the verbs in parentheses in the correct form.

Popcorn (1) _became_ (become) popular in the 1920s, when food prices (2) __________ (rise) during the Great Depression. It was cheap and (3) __________ (make) easily in large quantities after the invention of the first electric popcorn machines. However, the art of making popcorn (4) _________ (discover) by Native Americans thousands of years ago. Christopher Columbus (5) _________ (greet) in the Caribbean by men wearing necklaces that (6) _________ (make) of popcorn. The corn (7) _________ (use) in religious ceremonies, but the Native Americans (8) _________ (also eat) it. Columbus (9) _________ (buy) a few of the necklaces to take home with him.

6 **Rewrite the sentences beginning with the words given.**

a A friend is helping me with this exercise.
I am being helped with this exercise by a friend.
____

b My teacher will grade my homework.
My homework _________________________________
____

c My sister is cooking my dinner this evening.
My dinner _________________________________
____

d No one has ever given me a ring.
I _________________________________
____

e No one will force me to take an English examination.
I _________________________________
____

f I haven't opened my dictionary today.
My dictionary _________________________________
____

g A friend invited me to their house last weekend.
I _________________________________
____

Change the sentences to make them true for you.

PRONUNCIATION

1 **24 Listen to the words in the box. Is the underlined sound /s/ or /z/? Put the words in the correct column.**

~~always~~	~~ask~~	beliefs	cheese	dessert
extensive	fussy	invisible	loose	noisy
please	restaurant	these	this	

/s/	/z/
ask	always

25 Listen and check. Repeat the words.

2 **26 Listen to the recording and practice saying the following groups of words.**

a /sp/ spinach spoonful spread sports spill
b /sk/ skipped squeeze scale score screen
c /st/ steak stick stodgy strict stroke

VOCABULARY

1 **Match the sentence beginnings (a–f) with their endings (1–6).**

a He raised c He stuck e She clenched
b He held d She bent f She shook

1 her finger to warn me of the danger.
2 her knees to speak to the small children.
3 her teeth to fight against the pain.
4 his arms to protect himself.
5 his chest out to show his muscles.
6 his head up to show he wasn't scared.

a	b	c	d	e	f
4					

2 **Complete the sentences with the verbs in the box in the correct form.**

bend	clench	hold	~~raise~~	shake	stick

a A few eyebrows were raised when the first model appeared in a new Dior creation.
b She _________ her head and said "no."
c Don't _________ your tongue out – it's rude.
d The teacher _________ her hand up and waited for the class to be quiet.
e Can you touch your feet without _________ your legs?
f He _________ his fists and shouted in wild anger.

3 **Underline the correct words.**

Guy: I found a restaurant for tonight. They have a decent (1) **set** / **square** menu, but you can also eat (2) **à la carte** / **plain** if you prefer.

Lisa: Do they have a (3) **stodgy** / **vegetarian** menu? You know I don't eat meat.

Guy: Yes, they've got some really interesting (4) **regional** / **unique** dishes. It's all (5) **bland** / **organic** food, actually. I think you'll like it. They have a lot of fish (6) **dishes** / **food**, too.

Lisa: Are you sure it's OK? Not like the place with (7) **mild** / **paper** plates you took me to last time?

Guy: No, this is a lot more upscale. Their website says they specialize in the "subtle (8) **flavors** / **plates** of Lebanese cuisine."

27 Listen and check.

4 **Complete the text with the words in the box.**

dishes extensive flavor fresh light ~~menu~~ three-course

I often have dinner at a restaurant called "The Vineyard." Their à la carte (1) ___menu___ has a lot of local (2) __________ , with things like beef cooked in juice, but you can also have something (3) __________ , like a salad. The food is (4) __________ and the service is friendly. While I'm looking at the (5) __________ menu, I usually order a plate of sourdough bread. Have you ever tried it? It has an unmistakable (6) __________ . The portions here are big, so you won't need to order a (7) __________ meal unless you're really hungry.

5 **Complete the text with the phrases in the box.**

As a result In fact In other words Secondly ~~The first and most obvious reason~~ To sum up What is more

I don't understand why so many people still go to fast-food restaurants. We should do all we can to avoid them. (1) ___The first and most obvious reason___ for this is that the food they serve has very little nutritional value. (2) ______________ , in large quantities, it is positively bad for us. We are encouraged to buy mega-size portions of greasy fries and one-liter cups of sugary fizz.

(3) ______________ , every country in the industrialized world is suffering increased problems with obesity and heart disease. (4) ______________ , these so-called restaurants are selling this high-calorie, high-fat food to adolescents, who need a healthy diet.

(5) ______________ , this junk "food" is sold in polluting containers that cannot be recycled when they are covered in ketchup. (6) ______________ , a regular diet of burgers and fries with cola, ketchup, and ice cream destroys not only your health but also the planet. (7) ______________ , I think that fast-food places should be closed down as an environmental health danger.

6 **Complete the text with the phrases in the box.**

although consequently even though furthermore however ~~so~~ to sum up

The restaurant *Chez Marcel* is very busy, (1) ___so___ we had to book our dinner five weeks in advance. (2) __________ the restaurant has three Michelin stars, we did not enjoy our visit. The food was bland and the meat was overcooked. (3) __________ , the service was awful. We were given a table near the bathrooms (4) __________ we had booked a table by the window. The waiter ignored us for most of the meal. (5) __________ , we decided not to leave a tip. It was, (6) __________ , a truly horrible experience. (7) __________ , we had an even worse meal the following day.

7 ▶ 28 **Listen to the recording. Underline the numbers that you hear.**

a 1959 / 19.59

b 999 / 0.999

c $\frac{1}{100}$th / 100

d 23,302 / 23,032

e 1.8004465447 / 1-800-446-5447

f 2.1 / 21st

8 **Underline the correct alternative.**

a Tennis player Ana Ivanovic beat her young opponent six **love** / **zero**.

b My telephone number is three, **nil** / **oh**, seven, nine, one, eight, seven, seven, nine, one.

c Norway became independent from Sweden in nineteen **oh** / **zero** five.

d Four fifths is the same as **love** / **zero** point eight.

e The coldest recorded temperature on Earth is eighty-nine degrees below **oh** / **zero**.

▶ 29 **Listen and check.**

9 **Cross out four inappropriate collocations. The first has been done for you.**

bland food

bright lighting

overcooked customers

noisy customers

slow service

~~dark customers~~

chilled menu

the shrimp is bad

overdone steak

busy food

LISTENING

1 30 Cover the listening script on the right. Look at the three newspaper headlines and listen to the recording. Which newspaper story has the man been reading?

Speed Eater Suffers Heart Attack

New Rules For Fast Food

Chestnut Wins Hamburger Olympics

2 Listen again and answer the questions.

a How old is Joey Chestnut?
b How much did he win?
c How long did it take Joey Chestnut to eat 93 hamburgers?
d How many burgers did the second-placed competitor eat?
e How many hot dogs did Chestnut eat in ten minutes?
f What kind of sandwiches does he hold world records for?
g How many competitive eating competitions take place every year?
h How many people watched Chestnut win the championship?

3 Look at the listening script and find six verbs and phrasal verbs that mean "eat."

a w *olfed down*
b s__________
c g__________
d s__________
e g__________
f s__________

Husband: Hey, have you seen this?
Wife: What?
Husband: This story in the paper. About some guy who ate 93 hamburgers in eight minutes.
Wife: No!
Husband: It was the World Hamburger Eating Championships.
Wife: You're kidding.
Husband: No, seriously. Listen. "Joey Chestnut, 24, from San José, California, has taken the $20,000 first prize in the World Hamburger Eating Championships for the second year running. Chestnut wolfed down 93 Krystal burgers in eight minutes, ten less than the world record he holds, but enough to see off his closest challenger, Pat 'Deep Dish' Bertoletti, who could manage to swallow only 85 in the time available."
Wife: Sounds like a competition you would have a chance of winning.
Husband: It's amazing. This guy, Joey Chestnut, is ranked number one in the world by the International Federation of Competitive Eating.
Wife: The what?
Husband: The International Federation of Competitive Eating, and he's got a whole pile of world records. In ten minutes, he can get down 72 hot dogs, 59 peanut butter sandwiches, or stuff himself with 47 grilled cheese sandwiches.
Wife: He must be completely crazy, stuffing himself like that. Can you imagine what it's doing to his health?
Husband: Yeah, just think of all that stuff in his ...
Wife: Some people, I mean they'll do anything to get into the Guinness Book of Records™, but gorging on a ton of hot dogs ...
Husband: It says here that there are hundreds of these competitions around the US every year. It's on prime-time TV and everything ...
Wife: No!
Husband: "Ten thousand people watched the event in Chattanooga, Tennessee," that's what it says. They eat burgers and hot dogs, pizzas, chicken wings, fried asparagus - that's a weird one - and there's even a ...
Wife: Asparagus?
Husband: You know what? I think I'll go and see if I can find a clip or something about it on YouTube.
Wife: Oh, not now. Dinner will be ready in a minute. I'm almost done.
Husband: Oh, OK. Later then, maybe.
Wife: No need. I can just watch you scarfing down your dinner. As usual.

7 Escape

GRAMMAR

1 Correct the mistakes in the following sentences. In each sentence, remove one word only. One of the sentences is correct.

a The travel agent suggested ~~us~~ that we go to the Florida Keys for our next vacation.

b He assured to us that we would have a wonderful time.

c He explained us that it had won an award for its clean beaches.

d He also mentioned us that it had a fantastic nightlife.

e He convinced to us that it was this year's top destination.

f Finally, he persuaded to us to book it by offering a discount.

g The company confirmed us that there would be no price increases.

h One week before departure, the company announced us that there was a 5% price increase.

i They told us that it was because of a rise in airport taxes.

2 Complete the second sentence so that it has a similar meaning to the first.

a "I did too little, too late," he said.
He admitted doing too little too late.

b "Be very careful," she told him.
She advised ______ ______ ______ very careful.

c "I will return soon," he said to me.
He assured ______ ______ he would return soon.

d "It'll be easy!" he said.
He claimed ______ ______ would be easy.

e "Yes, I am married," she said.
She confirmed ______ ______ ______ married.

f "Go ahead! Buy it!" he said to her, pointing at the car.
He tried to persuade ______ ______ buy the car.

g "Go. Now!" she said to them.
She encouraged ______ ______ leave quickly.

3 Complete the second sentence with between two and four words so that it means the same as the first sentence.

a It wasn't necessary for me to travel far for my last vacation.

I didn't have to travel far for my last vacation.

b I was only allowed to take 10 kilos of baggage with me.

I ______________ take 10 kilos of baggage with me.

c It was necessary for us to book the vacation a long time in advance.

We ______________ the vacation a long time in advance.

d We couldn't pay by credit card.

We were ______________ pay by credit card.

e Fortunately, we were permitted to use my parents' car.

Fortunately, we ______________ my parents' car.

f We were not allowed to park the car outside our accommodations.

We ______________ the car outside our accommodations.

g It wasn't necessary for us to spend much money.

We ______________ to spend much money.

4 Complete the story with ***a***, ***an***, ***the***, or **-** (no article).

Mrs. Camilla Rust, of Seaford in (1) _the_ south of (2) ____ England, was shocked one morning to discover that (3) ____ gnome had disappeared from (4) ____ yard at (5) ____ front of her house, although (6) ____ other four were untouched. Ten days later, she received (7) ____ letter. In (8) ____ envelope, there was (9) ____ picture of (10) ____ missing gnome standing in (11) ____ middle of (12) ____ Colosseum in (13) ____ Rome. (14) ____ next day, (15) ____ second letter arrived with (16) ____ French stamp on it. This time, (17) ____ gnome was photographed on (18) ____ mountain in (19) ____ east of (20) ____ France. (21) ____ letters continued every day for (22) ____ month, with (23) ____ pictures of (24) ____ gnome in (25) ____ different parts of (26) ____ world. Then, (27) ____ letters stopped. One morning, (28) ____ week later, Mrs. Rust found (29) ____ missing gnome in its usual place in (30) ____ yard.

5 Correct the mistakes in these sayings.

a You can't measure the happiness.
You can't measure happiness.

b There never was the good war or bad peace.
____

c Friendship is love with the intelligence.
____

d Men never remember, but the women never forget.
____

e The money is power.
____

f Nothing is certain in the life except the death and taxes.
____

Do you agree with the sentences above?

VOCABULARY

1 Match the words in the box with the definitions.

advise	assure	claim	convince
mention	persuade	reassure	~~suggest~~

a offer an idea for someone to consider _suggest_

b give your opinion to someone about the best thing to do ____________

c tell someone that something will happen or that something is true, so that there is no doubt ____________

d make someone feel less worried about something ____________

e make someone believe that something is true ____________

f make someone agree to do something by giving them good reasons ____________

g say something in conversation without giving it much importance ____________

h say that something is true, even if there is no proof ____________

2 Choose the correct alternative: *a*, *b*, *c*, or *d*.

1 He _claimed_ that the New York Giants had won the cup in 1997, but nobody agreed.
a) advised b) claimed c) mentioned d) reassured

2 I can ____________ you that we will do everything possible to make your stay comfortable.
a) assure b) claim c) confirm d) explain

3 She accused me of lying, and I had to ____________ that I was.
a) admit b) advise c) inform d) mention

4 If you don't return the money, we will have to ____________ the police.
a) advise b) confirm c) inform d) suggest

5 It was easy to ____________ her to come with us.
a) admit b) announce c) mention d) persuade

6 The rumors were ____________ when the pictures were published in the newspapers.
a) assured b) confirmed c) convinced d) encouraged

7 You'll never ____________ me that she was innocent.
a) claim b) convince c) insist d) suggest

8 Why do you ____________ on speaking English all the time?
a) assure b) confirm c) encourage d) insist

3 Check (✓) the words which can be made into an adjective by adding the suffix ***-ish***.

a bull ✓
b child
c devil
d fool
e help
f hell
g humor
h pain
i self
j taste

4 Make adjectives by adding ***-ful*** or ***-less*** to the words in the box, and use these words to complete the sentences.

care	child	doubt	~~end~~
help	relent	stress	taste

a There was an ___endless___ line of people waiting to receive food.
b Be __________ with that – it's a dangerous weapon!
c Americans have a reputation for being __________ to foreign visitors.
d The food they serve is cold and __________ .
e The noise of the neighbors' arguments is __________ – they never stop.
f It's very __________ that you'll finish on time – you've hardly started.
g It was a __________ marriage, but they were very happy together.
h Some people say teaching is a __________ job, but they should try driving an ambulance.

5 Complete the sentences with the negative form of the adjectives in the box.

divided	~~legal~~	literate	logical
mature	polite	willing	

a Drugs like marijuana are ___illegal___ in most countries.
b To hide the fact that he was __________ , he said that he didn't like reading.
c He was more than __________ – he was extremely rude.
d She's still very __________, but she'll grow up soon.
e Unfortunately, the bank was __________ to help me.
f You may think that my decision is __________, but I can explain my reasons.
g I would like your __________ attention, please.

6 Write the missing letters to complete the text.

When you arrive in Bruges, you (1) sh_o_u_l_d go to the main square, Markt, and go into the tallest building on the square, the Bell Tower. It's (2) w_ _ _ worth the effort to climb the 350 steps to the top for spectacular (3) v_ _ _ _ over the rooftops and canals of the town. After that, I'd definitely (4) r_ _ _ _ _ _ _ _ a canal trip. The experience can be a little touristy, but you (5) w_ _ _ be disappointed if you choose the right time. It's probably best to (6) a_ _ _ _ the town altogether on busy weekends. In fact, if I (7) w_ _ _ you, I'd go in March when it's very quiet. (8) W_ _ _ _ _ _ _ you do, don't miss the "Begijnhof" – it used to be a home for religious women – which is beautiful in the early spring. Another (9) m_ _ _-see is the Memling museum, which is in a twelfth-century building. Oh, and make (10) s_ _ _ you buy some chocolate before you leave – the streets behind the Markt are the best (11) p_ _ _ _ to find chocolate stores.

▶ 31 **Listen and check.**

PRONUNCIATION

▶ 32 **Listen to the way the expressions in italics are pronounced. Notice the way the voice goes up on the stressed syllable, which is underlined. Practice saying these expressions.**

a *Actually*, it wasn't the best vacation we've had.
b *To tell the truth*, we were a little disappointed.
c *Basically*, we should have done more research before we left.
d *In fact*, we didn't book it until the last minute.
e *Anyway*, we tried to make the most of it.
f *Come to think of it*, there were one or two moments that weren't too bad.
g *In the end*, I think the children really enjoyed themselves.

WRITING

Writing a description of a place
Sentence frames

1 **Read the short article below and check (✓) the topics which are mentioned.**

a	cost	g	language
b	entertainment	h	local customs
c	famous inhabitants	i	museums
d	festivals	j	scenery
e	history	k	shopping
f	sports facilities	l	theaters

Baltimore

With a population of over half a million, Baltimore is bigger than Boston and Las Vegas, but it remains unknown to many visitors to the USA. The city suffered enormously in the 1980s, but there is more to this city than closed steel factories and the docks. Although you may never have considered it as a tourist destination, it is worth taking a closer look.

Incredible as it may seem, Baltimore (on the east coast of the USA) boasts one of the country's best aquariums, The National Aquarium. (1) If that doesn't appeal to you, then an excursion out of town is a must. The city is situated near the beautiful Chesapeake Bay, the largest estuary in North America. (2) But what really makes Baltimore stand out is its nightlife. This is a happening town – movie theaters, restaurants, clubs, and café-bars. (3) And all at half of the cost they would be in New York City.

Baltimore

For overseas visitors, Baltimore deserves to be high on their list of places to visit. (4) Forget Florida or California, where you won't get to see beyond the usual tourist attractions. Baltimore is the real thing. (5)

2 **Read the article again. In which numbered blanks in the article do these sentences belong? Write the number in the box.**

a Although you can still get your steak and fries, you're more likely to find people eating soft-shell crabs and drinking cold lemonade. ☐

b For those coming to learn the language, you can be sure of a warm welcome here. ☐

c This is the USA as it really is – not the theme park version that most people see. ☐

d Home to more than 660 species of animals, it includes a 4-D Immersion Theater. ☐

e Beaches, meandering rivers, and wildlife are just a stone's throw away. ☐

3 **Complete the following sentences so that they are true for your town or area.**

a There is more to ____________________
than ____________________
____

b ____________________
____
is particularly worth seeing.

c ____________________
boasts one of the most ____________________
____

d If that doesn't appeal to you, then __________
____
is a must.

e What really makes ____________________
special is ____________________
____

f If you do visit ____________________,
it's a good idea to ____________________
____

4 **Imagine you work for the tourist office. Write a short report (approximately 180 words) for visitors to your town or area.**

- Look at Exercise 1 and decide which topics you will include.
- Decide the order in which you will deal with these topics.
- Choose one aspect of your town/area to concentrate on for your final paragraph.

8 Attraction

GRAMMAR

1 **Report the statements using the verb in parentheses and a passive reporting structure.**

a They have had a fight. (think)
It is thought (that) they have had a fight.

b They are getting divorced. (say)
It ______________________________
____

c An announcement will be made tomorrow. (believe)
It ______________________________
____

d Frances has taken the children to Los Angeles. (suggest)
It has ______________________________
____

e William wants custody of the children. (say)
It has ______________________________
____

f Frances has fallen in love with a younger man. (believe)
It ______________________________
____

g They will be getting married in the spring. (think)
It ______________________________
____

2 **Report the sentences using the words given.**

a It is thought that chocolate relieves stress.
Chocolate *is thought to relieve stress.*

b It is believed that blondes have more fun.
Blondes ______________________________

c It is thought that gray hair is attractive in men.
Gray hair ______________________________

d It was said that pale skin was a sign of great beauty.
Pale skin ______________________________

e It was once considered that cosmetic surgery was an expensive luxury.
Cosmetic surgery ______________________________
____

f It is believed that brown eyes are stronger than blue eyes.
Brown eyes ______________________________
____

g It is known that working in front of a computer screen is bad for your eyes.
Working in front of a computer screen ______________________________
____

3 **Complete the second sentence in each pair so that it means the same as the first sentence.**

a I went for an eye test last week.
I had *my eyes tested* last week.

b Your bike needs fixing.
You __________ get your bike __________ .

c Your hair is way too long.
You should get __________ .

d We're going to ask the builder to knock down this wall.
We're __________ have __________ down.

e The company has decided to change its logo.
The company is __________ get its logo __________ .

f The mechanic checked the car last week.
We had __________ last week.

4 Use the words in parentheses to make correct sentences. Make any other changes that are necessary.

a If you find some money on the street, what would you do with it? (were to)
If you were to find some money on the street, what would you do with it?

b Would you have cosmetic surgery, you had the money to pay for it? (assuming)
____
____

c You could make a radical change to your lifestyle, what change would you make? (imagine)
____
____

d Suppose someone give you three wishes, what would you wish for? (were to)
____
____

e Who would you choose you were to get the chance to spend an evening with the celebrity of your choice? (supposing)
____
____

f What job would you like to do, money, time, and talent were no object? (assuming)
____
____

Write true answers to the questions.

PRONUNCIATION

1 33 **Look at the phrases below and listen to the recording. Notice how the stress changes.**

a He's very warm-hearted.
b He's a warm-hearted person.

2 34 **Listen and underline the stressed syllable in the following compound adjectives.**

a absent-minded
b big-headed
c easy-going
d good-looking
e level-headed
f open-minded
g self-centered
h laid-back

VOCABULARY

1 **Label the picture using the words in the box.**

cheekbone	dimple	~~eye~~	eyebrow	jaw

a *eye* ________ b ________ c ________

d ________ e ________

2 **Underline one noun in each group that can be described by the adjective in bold.**

a **smooth** eyes, nose, skin
b **white** lips, teeth, smile
c **sparkling** bone structure, eyes, dimples
d **square** cheekbones, jaw, nose
e **big** bone structure, skin, smile
f **turned-up** teeth, cheekbones, nose
g **high** cheekbones, eyebrows, lips
h **arched** dimples, eyebrows, teeth
i **full** lips, skin, teeth

3 **Which expressions from Exercise 2 *cannot* be used to describe the face in the picture?**

4 **Complete the description of the woman in the picture using words from Exercises 1 and 2. Use one word in each blank.**

She has a classically beautiful face. She has a beautiful, (1) *big* smile and wonderful, perfectly (2) ________ teeth. Her lips are (3) ________ and her skin is (4) ________ and clear. She has very good (5) ________ structure, with (6) ________ cheekbones and a pretty, heart-shaped face. She has (7) ________ in her cheeks, which add to the youthfulness of her expression, as do the softly arched (8) ________ and her bright, sparkling (9) ________.

5 Match the two halves of the adjectives.

a	self-	back
b	grown-	centered
c	laid-	headed
d	level-	minded
e	open-	to-earth
f	down-	up

6 Match the adjectives from Exercise 5 with the definitions below.

1 self-centered ______ : too interested in yourself so you don't think about what other people feel or need

2 ______ : calm and easy-going, not worried about problems and not easily stressed

3 ______ : behaving in a calm and rational way, even in a difficult situation

4 ______ : willing to consider new ideas, not having prejudices

5 ______ : practical and realistic, doesn't panic or react emotionally

6 ______ : looking or acting like a responsible adult

7 Complete the texts using the adjectives from Exercise 6.

a She's so self-centered. It's always "me, me, me" and she never listens to a word anyone else says.

b You know, I really don't think Donna is very ______ at all. She's always judging people and finding fault in everything they do.

c That wasn't very ______, was it? Do you think that putting glue on my seat is funny? I wish you'd act your age!

d He's so famous and so successful, but when you get talking to him, you realize he's really normal, ordinary, and totally ______.

e Jake is just so ______. He's great; he never, ever panics and always knows what to do in an emergency.

f He's so ______ he's half asleep! Nothing ever seems to stress him out.

8 Replace the adjectives in Exercise 7 with the adjectives in the box.

mature relaxed ~~selfish~~ sensible tolerant unpretentious

a selfish ______ d ______

b ______ e ______

c ______ f ______

9 Underline the correct adjective. In three of the sentences, both adjectives are correct.

a Jenny's really **caring** / **selfish**. She'd make a great nurse.

b Tom is just so cold and **stand-offish** / **unfriendly**. He never says hello and just walks away when I try to start a conversation!

c I think we need someone really **experienced** / **mature** for the job of project manager.

d One of the most important things for me in a relationship is trust. I need my partner to be totally honest and **trustworthy** / **dependable**.

e There's something very **level-headed** / **mysterious** about the way she behaves. It's as if she has something to hide.

f Her parents are so **straight** / **open-minded**. They don't know how to react to their daughter's strange choice of friends.

10 Replace the phrases in bold with one of the idioms from the box. Make any changes that are necessary.

a shoulder to cry on up to my eyes in work cost an arm and a leg made up my mind play it by ear get it off my chest from this neck of the woods ~~put my foot in my mouth~~

a Oh, sorry, did I **say something wrong**?
Oh, sorry, did I put my foot in my mouth?

b I really need to **tell someone what happened**.
______

c He finally **came to a decision**.
______

d They **don't live near here**.
______

e I just need **someone to show me their sympathy**.
______

f **I've got a ton of stuff to get done** today.
______

g Let's **not make any specific plans**.
______

h It **was really expensive**.
______

LISTENING

1 35 **Listen to Lara and Jake on a speed date. Check (✓) the topics that are mentioned.**

a	hobbies	✓	d	tattoos	☐
b	family	☐	e	jewelry	☐
c	friends	☐	f	travel	☐

2 **Listen again. Are the statements true (T) or false (F)?**

a Jake collects stamps. ☐
b Lara's father collects stamps. ☐
c Jake's father is a mailman. ☐
d Jake has a tattoo. ☐
e Lara hasn't had her ears pierced. ☐
f Lara doesn't like tattoos. ☐
g Lara has a tattoo. ☐
h Jake wants another date with Lara. ☐

3 **Listen again or read the script and find expressions that mean:**

a I'm joking
1 ______________________
2 ______________________

b You're joking, aren't you?
____

c I'm sure
____

d The same thing is true about...
____

e Wait a minute
____

f There's no time left
____

Lara: Hi, Jake.
Jake: Hello there, Lara.
Lara: So, Jake, tell me one interesting thing about yourself.
Jake: Interesting? Well, I collect stamps. I've been collecting stamps since I was about seven.
Lara: Stamps?
Jake: No, I'm just kidding ... do I look like a stamp collector? I mean, you know, stamps are about the most boring thing on earth.
Lara: Actually, my dad's a philatelist.
Jake: A philate - what?
Lara: A philatelist - he studies stamps; he works for the Smithsonian.
Jake: Oh, sorry, I just put my foot in my mouth, didn't I? I mean, you know ...
Lara: No, I'm just pulling your leg - he's a mailman, actually.
Jake: Mailman? Ha, ha - good one.
Lara: So, anyway, you still haven't told me anything interesting ...
Jake: OK ... well, I've got a tattoo of a Chinese lion in a very interesting place ...
Lara: Oh, yes? And where would that be?
Jake: Sorry, can't tell you, you'll have to get to know me a little better first ... Hey, *you* should have a tattoo done.
Lara: Yeah, what kind of tattoo?
Jake: I don't know. A flower maybe, or a bird ... I can't really make up my mind.
Lara: Yeah, well, the thing is, I don't really agree with tattoos - you know, I don't think we should mess around with our bodies like that ... and what about when you get older? I mean, will you still want a Chinese lion when you're in your 70s? The same goes for piercings ... I mean, they're OK when you're young ... but when you get older ...?
Jake: What, not even your ears? Come on, I bet you've had your ears pierced ... everybody's had their ears pierced ... Hey, hold on, you're pulling my leg again, aren't you? Let's see your ears? Pierced?
Lara: Yes. You were a little slow there, weren't you?
Jake: Yeah, OK ... OK ... don't you take anything seriously?
Lara: I try not to.
Jake: You know, you have very pretty ears - and I love your earrings.
Lara: Thank you ...
Jake: Are you sure you don't have a tattoo?
Lara: Well, yes, I do, actually. Look. Here ...
Jake: Oh, wow, that's really great ... It's so small, I didn't notice it. Let me take a closer look ... Oh, no, time's up. Can I see you again? I promise not to talk about stamps.

9 Genius

GRAMMAR

1 **Underline the correct verb in the mini-conversations.**

a A: Do you know where my smartphone is?
B: Yes, it's in the bathroom. You **must** / **couldn't** have left it there this morning.

b A: I'm finished.
B: You **couldn't** / **might** be finished already!

c A: Did I tell you about my friend Roger?
B: I think you **can't** / **might** have told me, but I've forgotten. Tell me again.

d A: I can't stop thinking about where he might be.
B: Yes, anything **could** / **must** have happened to him!

e A: My ex-boyfriend starred in a movie once.
B: Really? With looks like his, it **may** / **must** have been *Planet of the Apes*.

f A: I'm sorry, but I think I **couldn't** / **may** have been a little impolite to you yesterday.
B: Impolite? I thought you were really rude, actually.

2 **Think about the president or leader of your country and write five sentences about what he or she probably did yesterday. You can use the ideas in the box to help you.**

Good or bad day?	Meetings?
Time up in the morning?	Lunch and dinner?
Entertainment in the evening?	Time to bed?

a He/She may have ______________________

b He/She might have ______________________

c He/She could have ______________________

d He/She must have ______________________

e He/She couldn't have ______________________

3 **Find and correct eight mistakes in the texts. The first one has been done for you.**

Some people think that the CIA may have ~~kill~~ killed President Kennedy. They say that Lee Harvey Oswald couldn't been responsible for the shooting and the CIA may be have murdered him in prison as a way of stopping the investigation.

A survey in the US found that one in five people think that the Apollo astronauts must never have landed on the moon. They think that the film of the event must have being done with trick photography. Some people even believe that the government might have faked all the Apollo missions.

It has been suggested by some people that the US government could has made secret contact with aliens. A mysterious crash at the Roswell military airport in 1947 may have be an alien spacecraft. Since then, it is thought that the government may kept another 11 similar incidents secret.

Check (✓) the theories which you think might be true.

4 **Complete the sentences with *as if / as though, like*, or – (if no word is needed).**

a It looks ___–___ terribly complicated.

b It looks ________ a machine for peeling potatoes.

c It doesn't look ________ very practical.

d It looks ________ the machine is very slow.

e It looks ________ the man has been fixing it.

f It doesn't look ________ something that many people would want to buy.

g The man looks ________ very old.

h He looks ________ a professor.

5 **Correct the mistakes. Check (✓) the two sentences that are correct.**

a That seems like a very good idea. ✓

b He appears to being asleep.

c It seems if we've been here before.

d They are look like rain clouds.

e The local people all seemed like very friendly.

____

f I seem to get poorer and poorer every year.

____

g The bar looked as if cool, so we went in.

____

h You look as you've seen a ghost.

____

PRONUNCIATION

36 **You will hear these sentences twice, but they will be said differently. Each time you hear a sentence, decide if (i) or (ii) is the most probable continuation.**

a She may have forgotten.
- i But I don't think so. [ii]
- ii She often does. [i]

b I might have left them at home.
- i I'll get them later. [ ]
- ii Or they may be in the car. [ ]

c It may have been an accident.
- i But it didn't look like one. [ ]
- ii He wouldn't do it on purpose. [ ]

d It could have been the wind, I guess.
- i It was really strong last night. [ ]
- ii But it looks more like a car drove into it. [ ]

e He might have finished by now.
- i I'll call him to see. [ ]
- ii But it usually takes much longer. [ ]

Listen to the recording again and practice saying the sentences in the two different ways.

VOCABULARY

1 Complete the sentences with the words in the box.

contemporary	derelict	eccentric	hideous
run-down	~~shiny~~	sprawling	tough

a He liked to keep his car looking bright and shiny.

b The shopping mall is a little ______________, but they're planning to redevelop it soon.

c Charles prefers traditional architecture and hates most ______________ buildings.

d She was brought up in a ______________ part of the city, where there was a lot of crime.

e She looked very ______________, with her wild black hair and strange clothes.

f The town was absolutely ______________, with not a single attractive building.

g The squatters lived in a ______________ house, surrounded by other abandoned properties.

h The ______________ suburbs stretched as far as the eye could see.

2 Match the definitions below to words from Exercise 1.

a built over a wide area in a way that is ugly or not carefully planned sprawling

b very ugly __________

c empty, unused, and in bad condition __________

d in bad condition because money has not been spent on repairs __________

e modern __________

f strange and unusual __________

3 Underline the correct alternative.

a There is a **captivating** / **surviving** view from the top of the mountain.

b It was **drizzling** / **intriguing** outside, but I hadn't brought my umbrella.

c They **endured** / **existed** six years of prison before they were set free.

d There isn't much **spitting** / **incentive** for some people to find a job.

e He looked **overcast** / **enigmatic**, but very little was happening in his head.

f She was a **mere** / **mysterious** twelve years old when she wrote her first novel.

4 Complete the text with the words in the box.

after	at	During	From	Just	On
Over	soon	~~When~~	while		

(1) When Felix Lope de Vega y Carpio, usually known as Lope de Vega, was five, he could already read Spanish and Latin. He (2) ______ began translating Latin poems into Spanish, and he wrote his first play (3) ______ the age of twelve. (4) ______ then on, he almost never put down his pen.

(5) ______ the next fifty years, he wrote more than a thousand plays and hundreds of poems.

(6) ______ his youth, Lope spent some time in the army, and he had a short spell in prison. (7) ______ his release from prison, he was ordered to leave his native city, Madrid. He took his sixteen-year-old girlfriend with him and married her. (8) ______ a few weeks after his wedding, Lope de Vega left his wife and joined the army again. At the end of the war with England, he returned to Spain, to his wife, and to writing in Valencia. However, (9) ______ the death of his wife, he was able to return to Madrid, where he had a series of relationships and married a second time. It was (10) ______ he was in Madrid that he wrote his best-known works. He died in 1635, an old man of 72.

37 **Listen and check.**

5 **Match the sentence beginnings (a–f) with their endings (1–6).**

a Airbus developed
b I just came up with
c More than 10,000 people apply for
d The businessman set up
e The police officer said he needed to conduct
f The professor carried out

1 a great idea to save the world.
2 a full body search.
3 a prototype of the A380 Superjumbo in 2005.
4 patents every year.
5 experiments on his own students.
6 the company with his wife's money.

a	b	c	d	e	f
3					

6 **Complete the texts using the prompts in parentheses.**

Before writing *The God Delusion*, Richard Dawkins was famous for his books about (1) genetics (geneti-), such as *The Selfish Gene*. Both of his parents had an interest in (2) __________ (biolog-), and Dawkins studied zoology in college. After graduating, he worked as a research (3) __________ (scien-) on a project investigating how animals make decisions. Before retiring, he worked as a professor of (4) __________ (scien-) at the University of Oxford.

Steven Levitt, a Chicago (5) __________ (econom-), and Stephen Dubner, a New York journalist, wrote the multi-million best-seller *Freakonomics* in 2005. They apply (6) __________ (econom-) theory to a wide variety of odd subjects such as the Ku Klux Klan or the way that parents choose their children's names. You need a certain amount of (7) __________ (mathemat-) knowledge to understand the statistics, but this is a fun way to learn about (8) __________ (econom-).

Stephen Hawking was a theoretical (9) __________ (physic-) and applied (10) __________ (mathemat-) at the University of Cambridge. His book *A Brief History of Time* has sold nine million copies. Suffering from motor neurone disease, Hawking used all the latest (11) __________ (technolog-) advances to communicate his ideas.

7 **One word in each sentence belongs to another sentence. Rewrite the sentences with the correct words.**

a He turned the tight on the thermostat to zero.
b You can't turn it on until you've holder it in.
c How did people change channels before they invented dial controls?
d Make sure the lid's on place before you turn it on.
e Put a cup under the plugged where the water comes out and push the blue button, OK?
f Take the filter out of the remote and replace it after every cup of coffee that you make.

WRITING

Writing a story
Narrative tenses
Use of pronouns
Lexical variety: nouns

1 **Read the text below and choose the best sentence to end the story.**

a At a news conference later, Walters said that he had done it because "you can't just sit around."

b It was a helicopter belonging to the US Air Force.

c He had liked balloons since he was a child.

California truck driver, Larry Walters, was always wanting to be a pilot. The only way open for *him* to do *this* was to join the US Air Force, but poor eyesight made *this* impossible. He didn't give up and began working on a plan for his first flight.

He bought 45 weather balloons from a local store and had filled *them* with helium gas. He fixed *these* to his garden chair, *which* was in turn tied to his jeep. For this epic journey, he also purchased some tea, a parachute, and a two-way radio. When everything was ready, he got into the seat and cut the ropes attaching *it* to the jeep.

His scheme worked well, at least at first. But the balloons continued to lift him up until he had reached the altitude of 5,000 meters. Fortunately, he had bought an air-gun which he could use to burst the balloons. He managed to burst ten of them, but then, unfortunately, he dropped the pistol. By now, he panicked.

Walters' flying garden chair began to get dangerously close to Los Angeles International Airport. Jet pilots who were flying nearby were astonished to see the bizarre sight, but this was a potentially dangerous situation. An airport helicopter had eventually succeeded in bringing him back to earth.

2 **In each paragraph, there is one mistake with a narrative tense. Correct the mistakes.**

3 **In order to make a text more interesting, it is a good idea to avoid repeating words. Find synonyms in the text that are used instead of the following words.**

a scheme ____________________

b flight ____________________

c bought ____________________

d chair ____________________

e air-gun ____________________

4 **Look at the words in italics in the first two paragraphs. Who or what do they refer to?**

a him Larry Walters

b this ____________________

c this ____________________

d them ____________________

e these ____________________

f which ____________________

g it ____________________

5 **Read the story below and rewrite it, choosing an appropriate narrative tense for the verbs in parentheses. Where necessary, change the words in italics, using pronouns or alternative vocabulary.**

At the end of his act, the Argentinian magician, Professor Marvo, (ask) a male member of the audience who (sit) near the front to come on stage. *Professor Marvo* (hand) *the member of the audience* a gun and (ask) *the member of the audience* to shoot *Professor Marvo* in the face. *The member of the audience* (fire) the gun and *Professor Marvo* then (pull) the bullet from between his teeth.

The member of the audience (be) so impressed that he (take) another gun out of his pocket. While Professor Marvo (prepare) to leave the stage, *the member of the audience* said to *Professor Marvo*, "Catch this!" and (shoot) *Professor Marvo*. *Professor Marvo* was killed instantly. Even during the subsequent trial, *the member of the audience* could still not understand why Professor Marvo (fail) to catch the bullet.

6 **Write a short story which ends with the following sentence:**

It's hard to believe that anyone could have been so stupid.

Write approximately 180 words.

10 Sell

GRAMMAR

1 **Insert commas into these sentences where necessary.**

a The most expensive advertisement of all time which was for the drink Guinness™ cost $20 million.

b It was made by Nicolai Fuglsig whose other advertisements include the Sony Bravia advertisement.

c It is thought to be one of the most effective advertisements that has ever been made.

d One of the advertising companies which has had the highest sales worldwide is Dentsu, Inc.

e Castlemaine XXXX which is a kind of beer once showed 17 different TV ads on one channel in one evening.

f An advertisement that was made for British Airways had over 6,000 people in it.

g The longest advertising poster ever produced which was made by O'Canada Gear© in Alberta was over 332 m long.

h Eight songs that came from Levi® jeans ads have reached number 1 in the music charts.

i Guy Ritchie who used to be Madonna's husband has directed a soccer ad for Nike™.

j Nike™ which is one of the best known brands worldwide spent more than $1.7 billion on advertising in one year.

2 **Complete the advertising slogans with an appropriate relative pronoun.**

a the taste *that* bites

b for the girl ________ can't say no

c the man ________ has everything

d the perfume ________ they wanted to ban

e at a price ________ you won't find anywhere else

f a man ________ life has been devoted to one thing

g the face ________ launched a thousand ships

h an experience ________ you will never forget

i for those ________ time is precious

In three of these slogans the relative pronoun can be omitted. Which ones?

3 **Combine the two sentences to make one sentence with a relative clause.**

a *Quantum of Solace* was first released in the UK. *Quantum of Solace* is the 22nd Bond movie.
Quantum of Solace, which is the 22nd Bond movie, was first released in the UK.

b Many Bond fans enjoyed Daniel Craig's performance in *Casino Royale*. They are glad to see him back in the role of 007™.

____

____

____

c Olga Kurylenko plays the role of a Russian-Bolivian agent. She helps Bond in his search for revenge.

____

____

____

d Mathieu Amalric plays the role of the villain. Bond has to try to stop this villain.

____

____

____

e The title for the movie is based on a short story. The short story appeared in a collection called *For Your Eyes Only*.

____

____

____

f The movie is directed by Marc Forster. Marc Forster also directed the Oscar®-winning *Monster's Ball*.

____

____

____

4 Rewrite the following story. Include the extra information that is given below by using relative clauses.

One day, Philip K. Wrigley was sitting on a plane. During the flight, the man asked, "Why do you continue to advertise a chewing gum?" Wrigley quickly replied, "For the same reason that the pilot of this plane keeps the engine running."

- Philip K. Wrigley was the founder of the famous chewing gum company.
- The flight was going to Chicago.
- The man was sitting next to Philip K. Wrigley.
- The chewing gum was already the most popular in the world.
- Philip K. Wrigley was known for his wit.
- The plane was flying at 30,000 feet in the air.

One day, Philip K. Wrigley, who was the founder

5 Rewrite the sentences beginning with the words given.

a I wouldn't want to be written about in the popular press.

What I wouldn't want *is to be written about in the popular press.*

b He's only well-known in the north of Canada.

It's only ______

c I really hate the way that celebrities always sound so sure of themselves.

What I really ______

d Being on TV is the only thing that matters to some people.

The only thing ______

e I don't understand why people take her so seriously.

What I ______

VOCABULARY

1 Match the words in bold with the definitions (1–8).

a He **glanced** over his shoulder nervously.
b She lay on the bed **gazing** up at the ceiling.
c I had been **eyeing** the boots in the store for months before I finally bought them.
d As she went out, she **caught sight of** herself in the mirror.
e Stop that! Don't you know it's rude to **stare**?
f A good teacher can **spot** a talented child.
g It was then that I first **noticed** him, standing in the corner, looking over at me.
h I could just about **make out** the writing on the side of the bag.

1 see something for a short time
2 look at something or someone in order to form an opinion of them
3 look at something for a long time, for example because it is attractive or interesting, or because you're thinking of something else
4 look somewhere quickly and then look away
5 see someone or something with difficulty
6 become conscious of someone or something by seeing, hearing, or feeling
7 see something and be able to identify it correctly
8 look at someone or something very directly for a long time

a	b	c	d	e	f	g	h
4							

2 Look at the verbs in bold. Check (✓) the ones that are correct. Change the ones that are wrong.

a I **made out** his face for a split second as he walked past.
I caught sight of his face
b She **stared at** me across the room.
c I couldn't **glance at** the details in the picture because the quality was so bad.
d He was **eyeing** the watches in the store window.
e I **caught sight of** the rain through the window for ages, thinking about what I'd say to her.
f He's really good at **spotting** mistakes.
g I could just **make out** his face in the crowd.
h Shh! They won't **gaze at** us if we just stand here and keep quiet.

3 **Cross out the noun in each group that is *not* frequently used with the word in bold.**

a	**advertising**	agency	~~confidence~~	industry
b	**brand**	awareness	identity	tag
c	**consumer**	choice	cut	goods
d	**market**	conference	leader	research
e	**price**	image	index	war
f	**sales**	figures	rep	sector

4 **Underline the correct word.**

a There has been a 20% fall in consumer **products** / **spending** over the last three months.
b Can I see the price **list** / **rise**, please? I need to know how much this juice costs.
c The company made more than $20 million in advertising **revenue** / **executive** last year.
d The sales **team** / **targets** have been working incredibly hard this quarter.
e I don't believe in paying extra for a brand **loyalty** / **name** when you can get the same thing without a logo for half the price.
f They were forced to sell their house for much less than its real market **forces** / **value**.

5 **Complete the sentences with the words in the box. Make any changes necessary.**

care less	conjure up	epitomize	fiercely	fussy	haunting	heart-throb	nostalgically	rugged	~~stripped~~

a He ___stripped___, threw his clothes on the ground, and ran into the ocean.
b He's a really ________________ eater. He won't touch vegetables, and he hates fish.
c I really couldn't ________________ about what you think. I'm going to do it anyway.
d The world of advertising is ________________ competitive.
e Dior perfume ads ________________ all that is chic in French fashion.
f All the girls loved his ________________ good looks. He was a ________________ and a heart-breaker.
g The two old men sat on the bench and talked ________________ about the good old days.
h A young woman sat in the corner playing a ________________ tune on her flute, ________________ images of deserted beaches.

6 **Write the missing letters to complete the texts.**

In an economic crisis, a fast-food restaurant can be a real cash (1) c_o_w. People cut (2) b_ _k on eating out in expensive restaurants, and although a burger and fries is a (3) f_ _ cry from a romantic candlelit dinner in a fancy restaurant, it's much cheaper. Which means the burger bars and the drive-ins are (4) r_ _ _ng in huge profits, while everyone else is tightening their belts.

Product (5) p_ _ _ _m_ _t is a marketing tool. Products such as cars, wristwatches, drinks, etc. are "placed" in movies and TV shows as a subtle form of advertising. And when the movie is likely to be a box (6) o_ _ _c_ hit, the companies are willing to pay vast sums of money for the (7) p_ _v_ _ _ g_ .

In 2008, Chelsea F. C. became the first soccer club to (8) s_ _ _k_ a deal with YouTube to allow footage of soccer games to appear on the website. They made it (9) c_ _ _r , however, that the deal could only be made on (10) c_ _d_ _ _ _n that no live footage could be shown.

7 **Check (✓) the sentences that are correct. Put a cross (✗) next to the sentences that are wrong and underline the mistake.**

a I get <u>absolutely nervous</u> before exams. ✗
b That was a totally ridiculous thing to say! ✓
c His performance was very extraordinary.
d That was definitely one of the best movies I've ever seen. It was totally good.
e I'm sorry, but I thought that was really very boring!
f Have you seen this video clip? It's absolutely amazing!
g The movie was pretty disappointing, but the party afterwards was extremely fantastic.
h I was terribly disappointed by the reviews. They were really awful.
i That was some horror movie. I was very frightened to death.
j Did you think so? I was extremely bored stiff.

PRONUNCIATION

1 **How do you think the following words are pronounced in English?**

Adidas®	Chevrolet™	Coca Cola™	Heineken®	Levis®	McDonald's™	Nike™	Nivea	Nokia	Perrier	Speedo®	Slazenger	Volkswagen

▶ 38 **Listen and check.**

2 39 Listen to the recording. Which sentence do you hear first? Number the sentences *1* or *2*.

a My friend, whose mom is Cuban, is bilingual. ☐

My friend whose mom is Cuban is bilingual. ☐

b She bought me an expensive tie, which I didn't like. ☐

She bought me an expensive tie which I didn't like. ☐

c My brother, who lives in Rome, is a model. ☐

My brother who lives in Rome is a model. ☐

Listen again and practice saying the sentences.

LISTENING

1 40 Cover the listening script on the right and listen to seven short voicemail messages. Match them with the small ads below.

1	2	3	4	5	6	7
C						

A **CAR SHARE.** I'm driving New York to LA at the end of this month. Do you want to share gas expenses and company? Call Dan 854-6927.

B **GREENWICH VILLAGE.** Close to subway, restaurants, bars, etc. Medium room $250 per week, available now. Non-smoking female prefered. 212-831-5246.

C **FORD MUSTANG,** 2004, blue, 50,000 miles, well maintained, perfect condition. 1st owner. $15,000 or best offer. Tel 520-716-5097.

D **PROFESSIONAL CATERERS,** for all occasions. We offer a wide range of catering services, from basic buffets to wedding parties. For information Tel/fax 831-732-8440.

E **PROFESSIONAL CHILEAN MALE** seeks friendly international people to share an apartment starting December. 732-862-5791. Ask for Felipe.

F **RETIRED AND LONELY** salesman, but with warm heart, generous, and not too bad-looking for my age. Can I take you out? Tel 209-893-6613.

G **FILIPINA LADY SEEKS** domestic job, childcare, cleaning, ironing, daily or part-time. Good references. Please call 510-875-6047.

2 Listen again. Write the numbers of the calls next to the statements.

a The caller doesn't leave a number 3 , ____ , ____

b The caller doesn't give their name ____

c The caller is an older person ____ , ____

d The caller is going to try again later ____ , ____

3 Look at the script and find:

a Four ways of asking someone to return your call.

____

____

____

____

b Two ways of saying you'll call again.

____

____

c Three ways of explaining the reason for your call.

____

____

____

1

Um, yes, hello, my name's Mac, Mac Richards, and I'm interested in the car you've got for sale. Could you call me on my cell phone? The number's 520-894-1258.

2

Good evening. The name's Ferguson, Karl Ferguson, and I'm calling about your advertisement. Could you give me a quote for my daughter's wedding? Eighty guests, buffet dinner, the whole shebang, the very best you can do. Please call my assistant at 831-749-2598. Thank you.

3

Hello. This is Monika Redman here. I'm looking for someone who would be able to pick up my little ones from preschool on Tuesday and Friday afternoons. Do you have a driver's license? I'll call again later.

4

Uh, I've never done this before, but you sound like a gentleman. I used to be in sales, too, before I retired, that is, and I was wondering if, maybe, I could take you out. I never know what to do with my money since my Hershel died. It would be my special treat.
My name's Mary and my number is 760-423-7799.

5

Hello. I am Isabel, and I am also looking for some people with whom to share an apartment downtown. I am staying in the Ramada Hotel. Could you please call me back there? Thank you.

6

Dan? Hi, my name's Hannah, and I need to get to LA in a couple of weeks. Could you call me back? How much do you think it'll be? Oh, my number's 212-610-7450. Bye!

7

I'm calling about the ad. Can I come over to take a look at the apartment? Is it near Bleeker Street? Er ... I'll call back in half an hour, OK?

11 Student

GRAMMAR

1 Underline the correct verb form.

a How well do you think you **will do** / **are doing** on the exam tomorrow?

b I'm **failing** / **going to fail** the English exam if I **don't** / **won't** get some work done!

c Some friends **will come** / **are coming** over to my house tonight to study.

d Once the exam **has started** / **will start**, no one **might be** / **will be** allowed to leave the room.

e **Will anyone try** / **Is anyone trying** to cheat in the exam tomorrow?

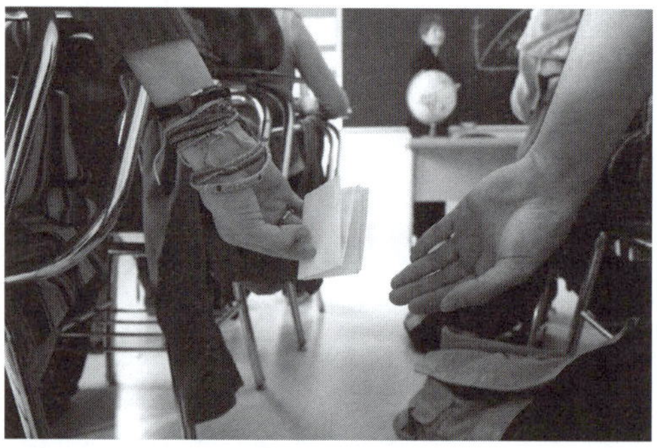

f They **will** / **might** – it depends if they get the chance.

g We **will have** / **are going to have** a party once the exams **will be** / **are** over.

h I **wait** /**'m going to wait** until I **know** / **will know** my grades before I go on vacation.

2 There is one mistake in each sentence. Find the mistakes and correct them.

a I'm going to study every single day until the exams ~~will~~ have finished.

b By the end of May I'll be finishing all my exams.

c I'm going to take some time off before I'm looking for a job.

d We're all going to go to Florida as soon as the semester is finishing.

e We might camp unless the weather will have changed.

f By July I will probably spend all my money.

g If my parents aren't giving me some money, I'll have to find a job.

3 **Complete the sentences so that they are true for you. Use the verb phrases in the box to help you.**

apply to college	buy a (new) car
finish my studies	get married
get a (new) job	travel
have children	leave home
move	get my driver's license
pass my exam	speak fluently

a I'm not going to ______________________ until ______________________

b By the end of the year I ______________________ ______________________

c I'll stop studying English when ______________________ ______________________

d I'll definitely ______________________ before I ______________________

e I'll ______________________ as soon as I ______________________

PRONUNCIATION

1 **Underline the word in each group that contains the vowel sound.**

a /ɪ/ last, least, list
b /i/ feel, fill, full
c /ʊ/ back, bake, book
d /u/ seen, soon, sun
e /e/ had, head, heard
f /ɜr/ lane, lean, learn
g /ɔ/ case, course, kiss
h /æ/ fan, fin, fun
i /ʌ/ bars, bees, buzz
j /ɑ/ heart, hot, hurt

41 **Listen and check.**

2 **Write the phonetic symbol of the vowel in the words below.**

a best ______ f school ______
b mark ______ g gap ______
c dream ______ h sort ______
d run ______ i good ______
e first ______ j thing ______

VOCABULARY

1 **Complete the text with the words in the box.**

applied	course	failed	grades
heart	higher	~~pay~~	scholarship

When I was in high school I just wasn't interested. I didn't (1) *pay* attention to the teachers and I was really bad at learning things by (2) ________ . I always got bad (3) ________, and there was no way I was going to go on to (4) ________ education. In my senior year, I (5) ________ all my exams, so I left school and got a job as a waitress. It was hard work, but I liked earning my own money, and after a couple of years I decided to take a (6) ________ in catering at a local college. I really enjoyed it and found that for the first time I was doing really well. So, at the end of the course I (7) ________ to college to study hotel management. I was so happy when I got in - and even happier when I got a (8) ________ ! Five years later and here I am, running my own hotel!

42 **Listen and check.**

2 **Complete the second sentence so that it means the same as the first.**

a It is not thought that he will study very hard.

It is unlikely (that) he will study very hard.

b He will probably fail most of his exams.

It is likely ____________________

____

c He'll definitely turn up without a pen.

He's bound ____________________

____

d He's sure to try and cheat.

It's inevitable ____________________

____

e He's likely to end up at the bottom of the class.

It's probable ____________________

____

f People don't think he'll go to college.

He's not expected ____________________

____

g He's unlikely to get a good job.

It's unlikely ____________________

____

h It's certain that he will get into trouble with the police.

He's bound to ____________________

____

3 **Write the missing letters to complete the expressions.**

a I got my first taste of freedom when I traveled on my own for the first time.

b It's always good to have a qualification b_ _ _ _ _ you.

c I really needed to travel. I just had to get it out of my s_ _ _ _ _.

d Have you come to your s_ _ _ _ _ at last?

e It's hard to m_ _ _ it in Hollywood.

f We can't really help her very much. It's all u_ t_ h_ _.

4 **Underline the correct word. Then match the expressions with the adjectives in the box.**

afraid	amazed	~~amazing~~	desperate	exhausted	happy	sad	sick	thirsty	worried

a It was **head-blowing** / **mind-blowing** amazing

b I was going out of my **mind** / **thoughts** ________

c I was in seventh **heaven** / **hell** ________

d I was on my last **breath** / **legs** ________

e I **fell** / **burst** into tears ________

f I was at the end of my **string** / **rope** ________

g It took my **breath** / **legs** away ________

h I was **dying** / **starving** for a drink ________

i I was at death's **door** / **gate** ________

j I was scared **solid** / **stiff** ________

5 **Write true answers to the job interview questions. Use the phrases in the box.**

always been interested in	ready/willing to	take steps to	very interested in	well-suited to

a What would you say is your greatest weakness?

____

____

b What are your greatest strengths?

____

____

c What would you like to be doing five years from now?

____

____

d What are your long-term objectives?

____

____

WRITING

Writing a job application email
Formal expressions
Appropriacy

1 **Find seven pairs of phrases in the list below which mean approximately the same. In each pair, mark one phrase *F* (formal) and one phrase *I* (informal).**

1 a (F) n (I) 5 ______
2 ______ 6 ______
3 ______ 7 ______
4 ______

a as advertised in the newspaper
b drop us a line soon
c I am not bad at
d I enclose my résumé
e I feel I am well-suited to this position because
f I have a good standard of
g I look forward to hearing from you
h I think it'd be cool to be a
i I would like to apply for the post of
j I've put in my résumé for you to take a look at
k my previous experience includes
l over the years, I have also
m the job looks just right for me because
n which I saw in the paper

2 **A job application email typically has four parts:**

1 reason for writing
2 factual information about the applicant
3 information about personality and interests
4 information about availability and conclusion

Decide which formal expressions in Exercise 1 would probably be in this type of job application email and which part of the job application email (1–4) they would be in.

a Part 1: Expressions ☐ ☐
b Part 2: Expressions ☐ ☐ ☐
c Part 3: Expressions ☐
d Part 4: Expressions ☐

3 **In the job application email extract below, cross out any information which would not be appropriate to include in a job application.**

I was born in a small town not far from Mexico City, so my mother tongue is Spanish, but I have a good standard of spoken and written English, because I have been going to an excellent language school near my town and I have been to the United States four times. I also had an Irish girlfriend for a couple of weeks.

I have an international driver's license, and I currently drive a red convertible Nissan™. I was going to work for a travel company here in Mexico last year, but in the end I worked for two months at the help desk at Mexico City Airport, where I had to deal with people from all over the world, and sometimes I got to drive one of the airport buggies if there was a disabled passenger who needed some help. It was fun.

4 **Look at the advertisement below.**

International Travel Organization

We are looking for young, friendly, and patient staff to work in July and August in LA. If you have the right profile, you will be responsible for meeting our clients at Los Angeles LAX airport and accompanying them to their accommodations.

No previous experience necessary.

Good level of English and one other language required.

Driver's license essential.

We offer a generous salary and will provide an apartment near our offices in Santa Monica.

If you are interested in this post, please send a résumé and accompanying a job application email to: Eleanor.gibbon@ITO.org

Make a note in the boxes below of information you would include in paragraphs 2 and 3 of your job application email.

Paragraph 2

Paragraph 3

5 **Write your job application email in approximately 180 words in an appropriate style.**

12 Home

GRAMMAR

1 **<u>Underline</u> the correct form.**

a I have a small desk by a window **overlooked** / **<u>overlooking</u>** the street.

b Out of the window, I can see a lot of people **walked** / **walking** down the street.

c In the kitchen, there is a picture of me **taken** / **taking** on vacation last year.

d I like to spend time in the living room **watched** / **watching** TV.

e The room, **cleaned** / **cleaning** only recently, is already messy.

f My bookshelves are full of unopened books **read** / **reading** by no one.

g I hate my bathroom, **located** / **locating** at the back of the apartment; it's very cold.

2 **Complete the text with the correct participle form of the verb in parentheses.**

(1) __Sitting__ (sit) in my penthouse suite on the 76th floor, I have a wonderful view of the city and of the ships (2) ____________ (go) up and down the river. My company headquarters, (3) ____________ (occupy) the other 75 floors, are conveniently placed under my feet, and the whole building is a landmark in the city, (4) ____________ (admire) by architects around the world. (5) ____________ (fit) with all the latest energy-saving devices, the building has won many awards. As I am the owner of a company (6) ____________ (specialize) in green forms of energy and (7) ____________ (know) for its interest in the environment, I am naturally very happy with my home.

43 **Listen and check.**

3 **Complete the text with the words in the box.**

all	enough	few	hardly	little	~~many~~
most	no	None	plenty	several	

There can't be (1) __many__ places as boring as my hometown. There used to be (2) ________ movie theaters and a (3) ________ youth clubs, but now there are almost (4) ________ facilities for younger people. Sure, there are (5) ________ of things you can do if you have a car, but you have very (6) ________ choice if you don't have wheels. There are (7) ________ any of my friends left - (8) ________ of them moved away when they had (9) ________ money. (10) ________ of them would ever go back there. Now that they are middle-aged, they (11) ________ seem happy living in a similar place on the other side of the country.

4 **Some of the lines in the text below are correct, and some have a word which should not be there. If a line is correct, put a check (✓) next to it. If not, cross out the unnecessary word.**

a Osgood, Indiana, isn't the most ~~of~~ exciting
b place in the world to grow up. There was not
c hardly anything to do and there weren't many
d other kids to play with. In any case, none
e of the other kids had much of time to play
f because they had to help their families, while
g I had way too much time. Ma had died when I
h was young, and Pop had no the time for kids.
i I dreamed of escaping to the big city and the
j several months after my 18th birthday, I left.

PRONUNCIATION

▶ 44 **Listen and repeat the phrases and notice how the underlined words are pronounced with a schwa sound /ə/.**

a get out of bed, the middle of nowhere
b leave at short notice, time at home
c a quarter to six, good to see you

VOCABULARY

1 **Complete the sentences with one word from Box A and one word from Box B.**

A

central	fireworks	fossil
~~go~~	pitch	street

B

cred	dark	display	fuels
heating	~~next door~~		

a I'm just going to __go next door__ for coffee.

b The world cannot afford to rely on ________________ .

c Bills for ________________ , both gas and electricity, are rising fast.

d He was a lot more interested in his ________________ than in doing his studies.

e The New Year began with a fantastic ________________ .

f Deep underground, the explorers found themselves in the ________________ when their lights failed.

2 Put the word tiles in order to make 10 breakfast foods.

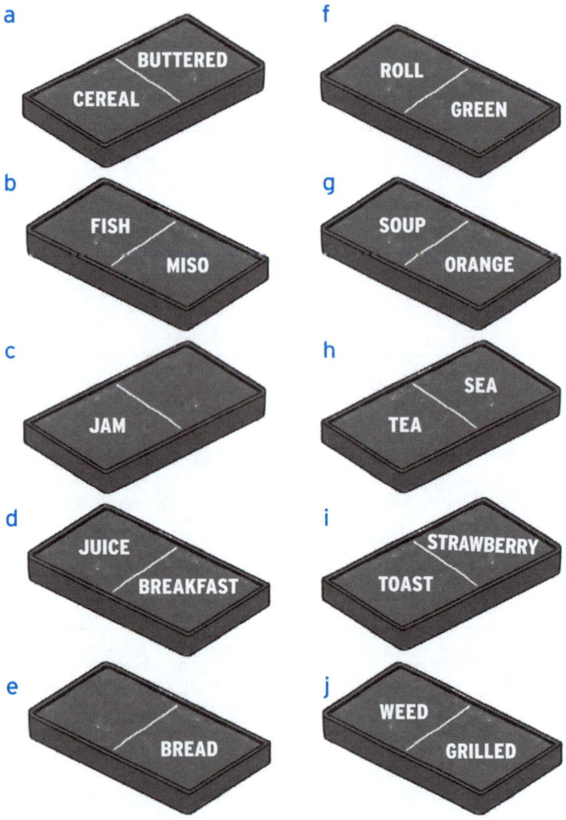

1	2	3	4	5	6	7	8	9	10
e	f								c

3 Number the lines in the correct order to make a conversation.

☐ Call me some time, OK?
☐ Good to see you, too. Thanks for coming.
☐ I will. Give my regards to Betty, will you? Bye.
☐ My pleasure. Thank you for inviting me.
1 Well, I'd better be going. It was really good to see you.

4 Complete the sentences with words from the word square.

D	O	O	R	M	A	T	S	I	L	L
J	R	B	R	U	S	H	U	M	Z	P
Y	N	T	I	L	E	S	T	C	K	C
M	A	N	T	L	E	P	I	E	C	E
D	M	L	N	C	S	A	L	B	L	G
U	E	A	F	P	H	R	R	O	B	L
S	N	T	O	C	U	Q	O	L	L	A
T	T	C	S	G	T	U	U	T	I	Z
P	S	H	T	Z	T	E	T	W	N	I
A	R	R	Q	F	E	T	L	E	D	N
N	M	P	L	L	R	Z	E	U	S	G
H	O	O	K	X	S	W	T	O	F	T

a A latch will keep the door shut.
b Some houses have s_ _ _ _ _ _ _ _ on the outside of the windows.
c You can use a d_ _ _ _ _ _ _ and b_ _ _ _ _ for cleaning.
d Most people's floors are covered with p_ _ _ _ _ _ _, t_ _ _ _ _, or wall-to-wall carpets.
e You wipe your feet on the d_ _ _ _ _ _ _ when you go into someone's home.
f Offices usually have b_ _ _ _ _ _ rather than drapes.
g Double-g_ _ _ _ _ _ _ keeps a room warm.
h Some people put flowers outside on the window s_ _ _ _.
i It's safer to slide the b_ _ _ _ across the door at night.
j You sometimes find a m_ _ _ _ _ _ _ _ _ _ _ with o_ _ _ _ _ _ _ _ _ on it above a fireplace.
k You can hang things up on a coat h_ _ _ _.
l You can plug in an electrical appliance at the o_ _ _ _ _ _.

LISTENING

1 ▶ 45 **Cover the listening script on the right. Listen to a radio feature about an auction in California and answer the questions.**

a What is being sold?

____

b How many people are taking part in the auction?

____

c How many different kinds of villas are on sale?

____

d In what ways are these properties "fully secure"?

____

e How much did the first property sell for?

____

2 Listen again. Are the sentences true (T) or false (F)?

a The auction is taking place in the center of Los Angeles. ☐

b The houses are in downtown Malibu. ☐

c People have to pay extra for things like swimming pools and saunas. ☐

d The male reporter would like to buy one of the houses. ☐

e People want to buy houses on estates that have high security. ☐

f Eleni thinks it will be difficult for some buyers to get a mortgage. ☐

3 Find words or phrases in the recording script to match the definitions.

a pushed or squeezed ______________

b connections ______________

c most fashionable ______________

d extremely rich ______________

e carrying a gun ______________

Auctioneer: Ten million dollars, eleven, twelve, thirteen, fourteen, fifteen, we have fifteen million dollars, and a half, sixteen, and a half, seventeen ...

Reporter: There are over four hundred people crammed into the auction house here in downtown LA where I am now standing. On top of that, it's believed that as many as four hundred more are following the bidding on the phone or on internet link-ups.

Auctioneer: Nineteen, and a half, twenty, twenty million dollars, twenty million, one, do I have two, twenty-two ...

Reporter: These are the first homes to be sold in a new residential development just north of Malibu, but what makes people ready to pay such prices? Well, there are four types of villas being sold today. Buyers can choose between the English country house, the Tuscan villa, the French Louis XIV chateau, or a Manhattan-style loft. All of them come with the basic necessities: swimming pools, jacuzzis, saunas, gyms, you name it. And they're all fully furnished, down to the smallest details: beautiful rugs from the best young designers, exotic indoor plants from the Honduran rainforest, or Picasso-inspired drapes. Despite the difficult economic times that we are living in, it seems that some people are not short of a buck or two. I asked Eleni Vassilakis, who is attending the auction, for her reactions.

Eleni: Hi. Yes, we're talking about some pretty serious real estate here. This is luxury for people who know what luxury is. To be honest, I'm not surprised that prices are so high here today. Remember that all of these properties are in a fully secure environment, the estate is surrounded by high walls and security cameras, and that's what people are looking for these days. Security is the word.

Reporter: The whole thing looks like a prison to me. I'm not sure I'd want to live there.

Eleni: Well, that's your choice, but I guess that you and I don't have that kind of money! We're seeing more and more of these estates, some of them guarded by dogs and armed security personnel, and they're proving very popular. These are not people who need a mortgage!

Reporter: From Malibu, California, this is Joe Wilson reporting on how the other half live.

Auctioneer: Twenty-six, that's twenty-six million dollars. Twenty-six. Sold. Now for lot number two, a Palladian-style villa with eleven bedrooms ...

Notes

Notes

Notes

Notes

Notes